COGAT®
GRADE 6 AND 7/8
TEST PREP

- **2 MANUSCRIPTS**
- **COGAT® GRADE 6 TEST PREP**
- **COGAT® GRADE 7/8 TEST PREP**
- **LEVEL 12, 13, AND 14 FORM 7**
- **352 PRACTICE QUESTIONS**
- **ANSWER KEY**
- **108 BONUS QUESTIONS ONLINE**

Nicole Howard

PLEASE LEAVE US A REVIEW!

Thank you for selecting this book.

We'd love to get your feedback on the website where you purchased this book.

By leaving a review, you give us the opportunity to improve our work.

Nicole Howard and the SkilledChildren.com Team

www.skilledchildren.com

TABLE OF CONTENTS

INTRODUCTION

The Cognitive Abilities Test (CogAT®) is an assessment of a student's verbal, quantitative, and nonverbal reasoning ability, designed to identify gifted students.

Riverside Publishing has developed the Cognitive Abilities Test since 1954.

These books will increase the student's chances of success by providing an overview of the different types of questions for Grades 6 and 7/8, Level 12 and 13/14, Form 7 of the CogAT® test.

Two practice tests (one for grade 6, one for grade 7/8) and their answer key, with clear explanations, are all included in each book to allow students to understand the testing structure and the different types of questions within it.

Additionally, by reading these books, you gain free online access to 108 bonus practice questions. You will find the link and password on the last page of each book.

It is highly recommended to read this introductory section to understand how the CogAT® works.

Which Students Are Eligible for the Levels 12/13/14?

This book is dedicated to gifted 12/13/14-year-old children and therefore focuses on levels 12/13/14, form 7 of CogAT®. These tests will determine whether specific grades 6/7/8 students are ready to take the test.

Most Grade 12/13/14 teachers implement CogAT® Level 12/13/14 to identify which of their students will benefit from faster curriculum training modules. Used as a starting evaluation, these tests deliver reasonably accurate results.

When in the School Year Does the CogAT® Take Place?

Several school districts choose to implement these tests at the end of the school year for more reliable and accurate results. If you are the parent or teacher of a student who could potentially qualify for this test, you will probably need to consult your school to determine how to enroll a child for this test.

An Overview of the CogAT® Level 12/13/14

The CogAT® is administered to a group of students at a single time.

There are three autonomous sections of the test, specifically:

1. Verbal testing

2. Nonverbal testing

3. Quantitative testing

These autonomous sections can be used individually, and some students may only be asked to take one or two parts of the test based on the evaluations of their tutors.

Although there are resources that support students prepare for these tests, the content of the CogAT® isn't generally the same content that is seen in the conventional school curriculum, and students will be asked to think creatively to solve certain questions.

The Length and the Complete Format of the Test

The total time given for the three sections of the Level 12/13/14 test is 90 minutes (30 minutes for each section).

Tests will vary, depending on the grades that are being assessed, but the Levels 12/13/14 of CogAT® are divided into 176 multiple-choice questions. The questions are categorized as follows:

Verbal Section

- "Sentence completion" has 20 questions.

- "Verbal classification" has 20 questions.

- "Verbal analogies" has 24 questions.

Nonverbal Section

- "Figure matrices" has 22 questions.

- "Paper folding skills" has 16 questions.

- "Figure classifications" has 22 questions.

Quantitative Section

- "Understanding number analogies" has 18 questions.

- "The number series" has 18 questions.

- "Solving number puzzles" has 16 questions.

The total number of questions for these three sections equals 176 for grade 6 and 176 for grade 7/8.

The Test Breakdown

The verbal section of the test is designed to assess a student's vocabulary, ability to solve problems associated with vocabulary, ability to determine word relationships, and their overall memory retention. The verbal section of the Levesl 12 and 13/14 of CogAT® have three subtypes of questions that need to be answered:

1. Sentence Completion: Students are required to select words that accurately complete sentences in this section. This tests their knowledge of vocabulary.

2. Verbal Classification: Students are required to classify words into like groups in this section. They will be given three words that have something in common, and will be asked to identify a fourth word that completes the set. Each question in this section will have five possible answers for the students to choose from.

3. Verbal Analogies: Students are required to identify analogies. They will be given two words that go together (e.g. "dog" and "mammal") as well as a third, unrelated word. They must pick the most fitting pair for the third word from the answer choices given, based on the logic used for the original pair of words.

The nonverbal section of the test is designed to assess a student's ability to reason and think beyond what they've already been taught. This section includes geometric shapes and figures that aren't normally seen in the classroom. This will force the students to use different methods to try and solve problems. There are also three subtypes of questions that need to be answered in the nonverbal section of the CogAT®:

1. Figure Classification: Students are required to analyze three similar figures and apply the next appropriate figure to complete the sequence in this section.

2. Figure Matrices: Students are introduced to basic matrices (2x2 grids) to solve for the missing shapes within them. Three of the four squares will already be filled out, and they must choose which image fills the last square

from the options provided. This is similar to the verbal analogies section, except it is now done using shapes instead of words.

3. Paper Folding Skills: Students are introduced to paper folding and will need to ascertain where punched holes in a folded piece of paper would be after the paper is unfolded.

The quantitative section introduces abstract reasoning and problem-solving skills to learners and is one of the most challenging sections in the test. This section is also structured into three different parts:

1. Interpreting a Series of Numbers: Students are required to determine which number or numbers are needed to complete a series that follows a specific pattern.

2. Solving Number Puzzles: Students will need to solve number puzzles and simple equations. They will be provided with equations that are missing a number.

3. Understanding Number Analogies: Students are introduced to number analogies and will be required to determine what numbers are missing from the number sets. This is similar to figure matrices and verbal analogies.

How to Use the Content in These Books

Since the CogAT® is an important test in all students' schooling careers, the correct amount of preparation must be performed. Students that take the time to adequately prepare will inevitably do better than students that don't.

These books will help you prepare your student(s) before test day and will expose them to the format of the test so they'll know what to expect. These books include:

- One full-length CogAT® Level 12 practice questionnaire.

- One full-length CogAT® Level 13/14 practice questionnaire.

- Question examples for teachers/parents to help their students approach all of the questions on the test with confidence and determination.

- Answer key for each book with clear explanations.

Take the time to adequately go through all of the sections to fully understand how to teach this information to younger students. Many of the abstract versions of these questions will be difficult for some students to understand, so including some visual aids during preparation times will be greatly beneficial.

Tips and Strategies for Test Preparation

The most important factor regarding the CogAT® is to apply the time and effort to the learning process for the test and make the preparation periods as stress-free as possible. Although everyone will experience stress in today's world, being able to cope with that stress will be a useful tool. All students will experience varying amounts of anxiety and stress before these types of tests, but one of the ways to adequately combat this is by taking the time to prepare for them.

The CogAT® has difficult questions from the very beginning. Some of the questions will range from difficult to very abstract, regardless of the age group or level.

It's necessary to encourage your students to use different types of strategies to answer questions that they find challenging.

Students will get questions incorrect in some of the sections, so it's vital to help younger students understand what errors they made so they can learn from their mistakes.

Before You Start Test Preparation

There are multiple factors that may stress students out, regardless of their age and maturity levels. It's imperative for you as an educator to help your students cope with the anxiety and stress of upcoming tests. The tests themselves are going to be stressful, but there are other, external factors that can increase the amounts of stress that children experience.

INTRODUCTION

The first aspect that needs to be focused on is teaching the learners how to deal with stress. Breathing techniques are important, and having a quiet place to use when studying is imperative to decreasing the amount of stress that students experience.

There are other aspects that can help alleviate stress, like teaching your students what pens and pencils they need to bring on the test day and how to successfully erase filled out multiple-choice questions on the test questionnaire.

COGAT® TEST PREP GRADE 6

VERBAL BATTERY GRADE 6

This section is designed to assess a student's vocabulary, ability to solve problems associated with vocabulary, ability to determine word relationship and memory retention.

Verbal Analogies

A verbal analogy traces a similarity between a pair of words and another pair of words.

Example

turtle → reptile : bee →

A insect   **B** reptile   **C** mammal   **D** fish   **E** amphibian

- First, identify the relationship between the first pair of words.
- How do the words "turtle" and "reptile" go together?

Scientists have classified the animals into classes to simplify their study.

Turtles are Reptiles. "Reptile" is a category.

- Now, look at the word "bee".
- Which of the possible choices follows the previous rule?

Bee is an insect, so the correct answer is A.

Tips for Solving Verbal Analogies

- Try to identify the correlation between the first two words.
- Review all answers before you make a choice.
- Remove any word in the answers that don't have a comparable kind of relationship.
- Also, evaluate the possible alternative meanings of the words.

1.

crying → sorrow : laughing →

A happiness   **B** tears   **C** disease   **D** comedy
E drama

2.

bout → about: mend→

A tear   **B** amend   **C** dismiss   **D** near   **E** big

3.

warm → hot : amusing →

A different   **B** leg   **C** hilarious   **D** cold   **E** hard

4.

crumb → bread : splinter →

A butter   **B** mountain   **C** wood   **D** fire
E moon

5.
album → photographs : shelf →

A pen   **B** paper   **C** toys   **D** cups   **E** books

6.
atlas → map : cookbook →

A recipe   **B** prescription   **C** letter   **D** poem
E fable

7.
football → sport : biology →

A flower   **B** music   **C** science   **D** metal   **E** poem

8.
anonymous → name : formless →

A table   **B** book   **C** cloud   **D** shape   **E** importance

9.

paw → dog : arm →

A man   **B** bear   **C** bird   **D** car   **E** umbrella

10.

infection → antibiotic : headache →

A toxin   **B** cake   **C** aspirin   **D** plant   **E** juice

11.

push → pull : throw →

A drink   **B** jump   **C** pick   **D** collect   **E** buy

12.

club → member : troupe →

A student   **B** child   **C** priest   **D** nun   **E** actor

13.

Moon → satellite: Earth →

A solar system   **B** sun   **C** planet   **D** asteroid
E light

14.

forecast → future : regret →

A past   **B** present   **C** tomorrow   D month
E year

15.

influenza → virus: typhoid →

A bacillus   **B** bacteria   **C** parasite   **D** spider
E protozoa

16.

thermometer → temperature: clock →

A energy   **B** radiation   **C** rain   **D** wind
E time

17.

scribble → write : stutter →

A play   **B** speak   **C** dance   **D** walk   **E** swim

18.

car → garage : airplane →

A port   **B** depot   **C** hangar   **D** house   **E** heaven

19.

acting → theatre : gambling →

A casino   **B** bar   **C** restaurant   **D** club
E cinema

20.

planet → orbit : projectile →

A track   **B** trajectory   **C** path   **D** street
E sky

21.

asylum → refuge : dungeon →

A remorse **B** labyrinth **C** classroom **D** death
E confinement

22.

drill → bore : sieve →

A sing **B** thresh **C** eat **D** sift **E** rinse

23.

import → export : expenditure →

A revenue **B** deficit **C** debt **D** credit **E** tax

24.

poodle → dog : moose →

A duck **B** donkey **C** deer **D** cat **E** bear

Verbal Classification

Verbal classification questions ask the student to choose the voice that belongs to a group of three words.

Example

king, queen, knight

A mayor   **B** nun   **C** pope   **D** minister   **E** bishop

- First, identify the relationship between the first pair of words.
- What do the words king, queen and knight have in common?

king, queen and knight are chess pieces.

- Now, look at the five worlds: mayor, nun, pope, minister, bishop. Which word goes best with the three words in the top row?

Bishop is also a chess piece, so the correct answer is E.

Tips for Solving Verbal Classification Questions

- Try to identify the correlation between the three words in the top row.
- Review all answers before you make a choice.
- Remove every word in the answers that don't have any kind of relationship with the three words in the top row.
- Also, evaluate the possible alternative meanings of the words.

1.

tooth, nose, eye

A ear   **B** neck   **C** arm   **D** hand   **E** leg

2.

clove, cinnamon, pepper

A apricot   **B** pear   **C** apple   **D** banana
E oregano

3.

zinc, iron, copper

A hydrogen   **B** helium   **C** nitrogen   **D** oxygen
E aluminum

4.

parsley, basil, dill

A oregano   **B** mayonnaise   **C** vinegar   **D** oil
E butter

5.

clams, oysters, scallops

A crabs **B** lobsters **C** mussels **D** sharks
E turkeys

6.

snake, duck, tortoise

A dolphin **B** shark **C** dog **D** squirrel **E** whale

7.

eyes, kidneys, ears

A heart **B** brain **C** lungs **D** nose **E** colon

8.

arc, diameter, radius

A diagonal **B** chord **C** square **D** triangle
E rhombus

9.

rose, lotus, marigold

A petal   **B** leaves   **C** corolla   **D** calyx
E tulip

10.

duck, crocodile, frog

A chicken   **B** dog   **C** pelican   **D** bat   **E** mouse

11.

coffee, milk, tea

A gold   **B** wool   **C** oxygen   **D** water   **E** silver

12.

curd, butter, cheese

A oil   **B** vinegar   **C** cream   **D** coffee   **E** tomato

13.
fingers, palm, thumb

A knee   **B** phalanges   **C** elbow   **D** shoulder
E mouth

14.
polyester, terylene, nylon

A cotton   **B** linen   **C** canvas   **D** jute
E spandex

15.
microscope, telescope, periscope

A stethoscope   **B** camera   **C** compass   **D** purifier
E thermometer

16.
cry, sob, weep

A laugh   **B** enjoy   **C** moan   **D** dance
E celebrate

17.

medium, average, mediocre

A terrible　**B** new　**C** high　**D** awesome
E intermediate

18.

honest, intelligent, wise

A stingy　**B** generous　**C** tattler　**D** spendthrift
E　thief

19.

basket, purse, bag

A hat　**B** trousers　**C** backpack　**D** scarf　**E** tie

20.

raid, attack, ambush

A defence　**B** protection　**C** resistance　**D** assault
E fortification

Sentence Completion

Complete the phrase using the appropriate word that best fits the meaning of the sentence as a whole.

Example

The cat was _____ outside the door.

A barking   **B** meowing   **C** loving   **D** dancing   **E** neighing

- First, read the sentence. You will realize that one word is missing.
- Look at the answer choices under the main sentence. Which word would go better in the phrase?

Meow= the crying sound a cat makes. Therefore, the right choice is "B".

Tips for Sentence Completion

- First, read the incomplete phrase.
- Think about what type of word you can use and try to anticipate the answer.
- Remove every word in the answers that don't have any kind of relationship with the main sentence.
- Read the incomplete sentence again.

1.

Her heart began to pound frantically, as if she were having a _____ attack.

A panic **B** joy **C** sleep **D** boredom **E** sadness

2.

The computer keyboard is _____ to put less strain on your wrists.

A colored **B** broken **C** shaped **D** beloved
E scheduled

3.

Researchers _____ that this group was at a higher risk of heart disease.

A calculated **B** constructed **C** spent **D** drew
E demolished

4.

The power supply should be connected by a _____ electrician.

A new   **B** qualified   **C** old   **D** wise   **E** brave

5.

In order to understand how the human body works, you need to have some _____ of chemistry.

A order   **B** license   **C** knowledge   **D** love   **E** hope

6.

Most airlines base their _____ lists on the cost of the individual ticket.

A waiting   **B** new   **C** passive   **D** future   **E** past

7.

Public companies have to _____ an annual report and accounts.

A sell   **B** publish   **C** buy   **D** tell   **E** command

8.

The government has _____ plans to improve the quality of primary school education.

A saved   **B** deleted   **C** afforded   **D** sold
E announced

9.

The police do not use force when arresting people unless it's absolutely _____

A profitable   **B** necessary   **C** destructive
D deleterious   **E** favorable

10.

I suspect that 10 years after the book is published, _____ will even remember the name of the author.

A children   **B** students   **C** nobody   **D** all
E many

11.

She forced herself to go out, knowing that she would feel more _____ if she stayed at home.

A happy   **B** motivated   **C** excited   **D** depressed
E wise

12.

Scientists first _____ the idea of the atomic bomb in the 1930s.

A conceived   **B** destroyed   **C** bought   **D** sold
E folded

13.

Global _____ will have serious consequences for the environment.

A happiness   **B** depression   **C** warming   **D** union
E creation

14.

The choice of methods for a particular study will _____ on the nature of the task and the resources available.

A create   **B** weigh   **C** depend   **D** active   **E** sell

15.

The doctor admitted that he didn't yet _____ the nature of Julie's illness.

A love   **B** create   **C** pray   **D** understand
E color

16.

Even if you have the _____ to take you to the top, there's no guarantee you'll get there.

A impudence   **B.** silliness   **C** defect   **D** talent
E weakness

17.

You can't divide a prime number by any _____ number, except 1.

A other   **B** old   **C** prime   **D** previous   **E** great

18.

Doctors usually explain the _____ of the treatment to patients.

A color   **B** words   **C** conversations   **D** risks
E pills

19.

A poor diet in childhood can _____ to health problems later in life.

A decrease   **B** lead   **C** cut   **D** support   **E** reject

20.

We're trying to _____ by eating at home instead of going out for meals.

A buy   **B** economize   **C** grow   **D** sell   **E** pay

NON VERBAL BATTERY GRADE 6

This section is designed to assess a student's ability to reason and think beyond what they've already been taught. This section includes geometric shapes and figures that aren't normally seen in the classroom.

Figure Matrices

Students are provided with a 2X2 matrix with the image missing in one cell. They have to identify the relationship between the two spatial shapes in the upper line and find a fourth image that has the same correlation with the left shape in the lower line.

Example

In the upper left box, the image shows a white circle with two diagonals.
The upper right box shows a white circle.
In the lower left box, the image shows a white square with two diagonals.Which answer choice would go with this image in the same way as the upper images go together?

The image of the answer choice must show a white square without diagonals. The right answer is "B".

Tips for Figure Matrices

- Consider all the answer choices before selecting one.
- Try to use logic and sequential reasoning.
- Eliminate the logically wrong answers to restrict the options.
- Train yourself to decipher the relationship between different figures and shapes.

1.

2.

3.

4.

5.

6.

7.

A   B   C   D   E

8.

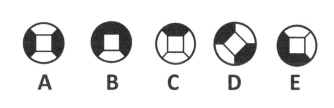

A   B   C   D   E

9.

A   B   C   D   E

10.

11.

12.

13.

14.

15.

16.

17.

18.

19.

20.

21.

22.

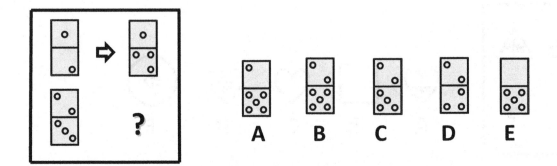

Figure Classification

Students are provided with three shapes and they have to select the answer choice that should be the fourth figure in the set, based on the similarity with the other three figures. The intention is to test the student's ability to recognize similar patterns and to make a rational choice.

Example

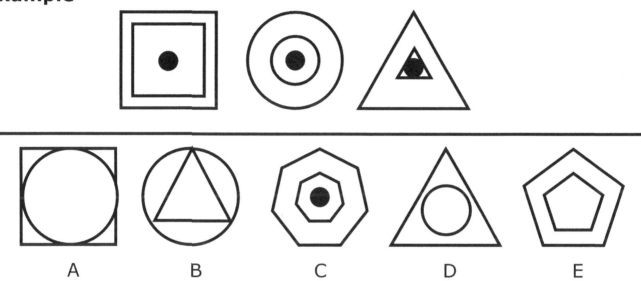

A   B   C   D   E

Look at the three pictures on the top. What do these three figures have in common?

You can see a black dot in a square in a bigger square, a black dot in a circle in a bigger circle, a black dot in a triangle in a bigger triangle.

Now, look at the shapes in the row of the answer choices. Which image matches best the three shapes in the top row?

The image of the answer choice must show two identical figures, the smaller one inside the larger one and a black dot inside the smaller one. The right answer is "C" (a smaller heptagon in a larger heptagon and a black dot inside the smaller heptagon.)

Tips for Figure Classification

- Be sure to review all answer choices before selecting one.
- Try to use logic and sequential reasoning.
- Try to exclude the obviously wrong options to reduce the answer choices.

1.

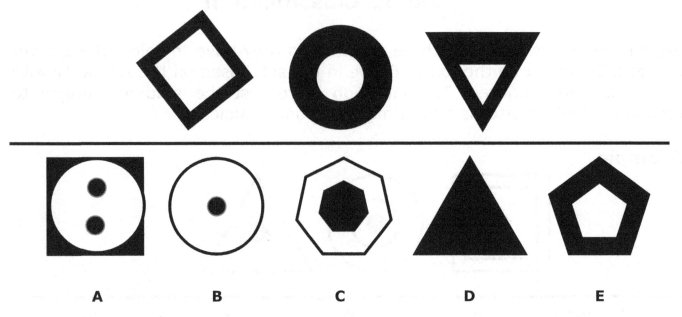

A   B   C   D   E

2.

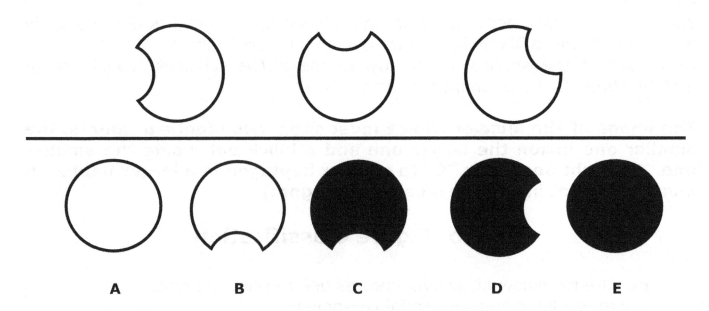

A   B   C   D   E

3.

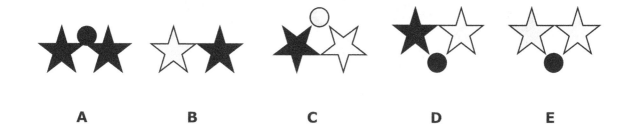

A	B	C	D	E

4.

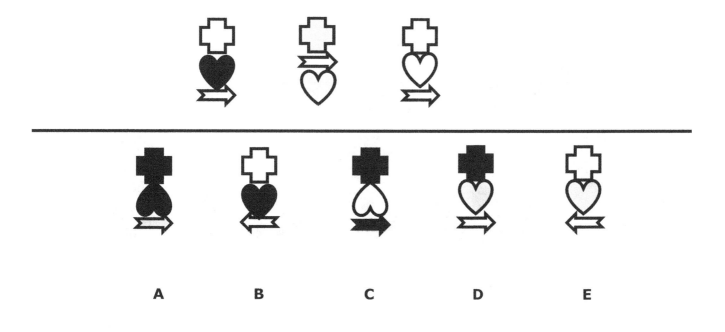

A	B	C	D	E

5.

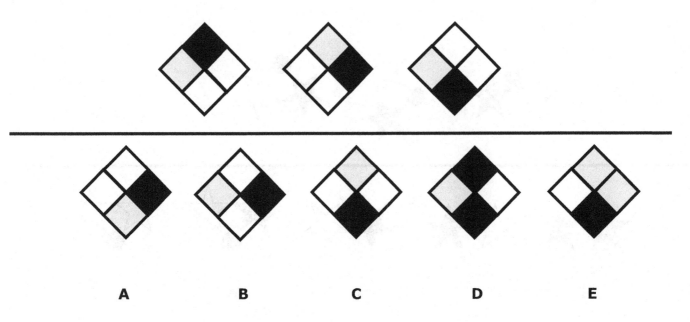

A   B   C   D   E

6.

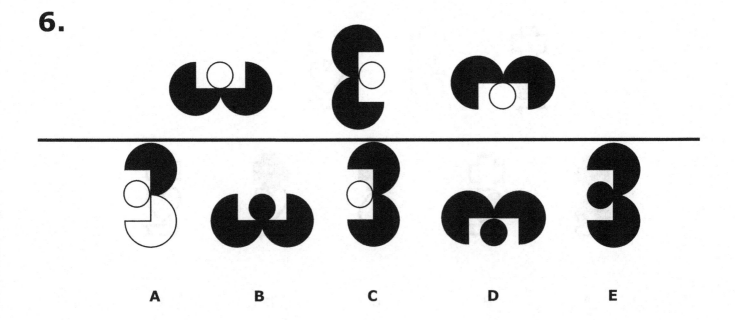

A   B   C   D   E

7.

8.

9.

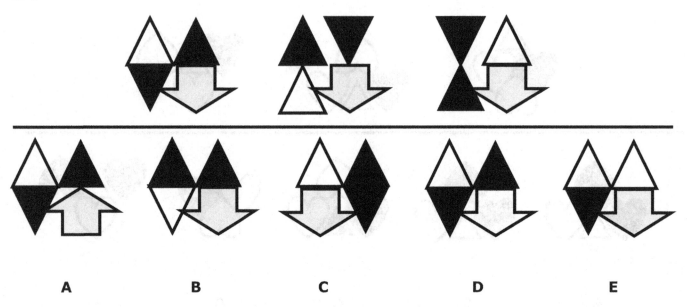

A   B   C   D   E

10.

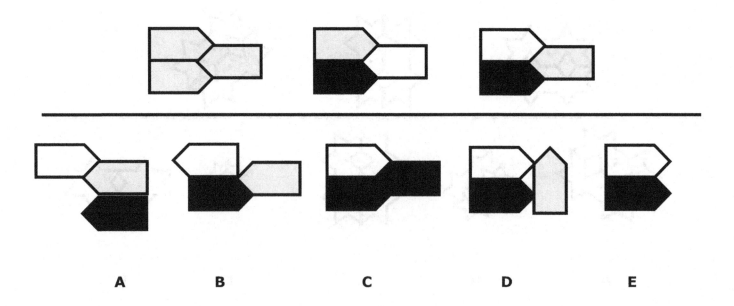

A   B   C   D   E

11.

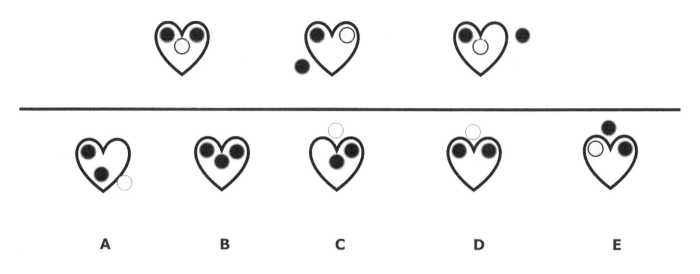

A   B   C   D   E

12.

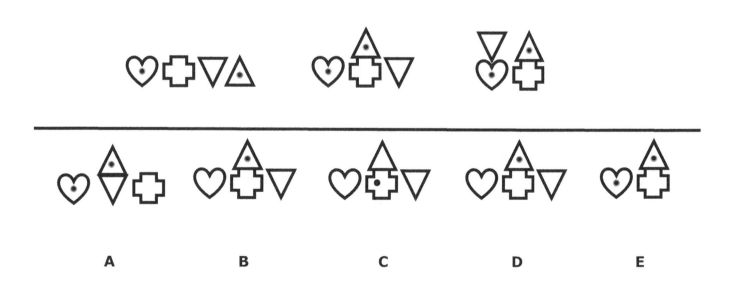

A   B   C   D   E

13.

14.

15.

16.

17.

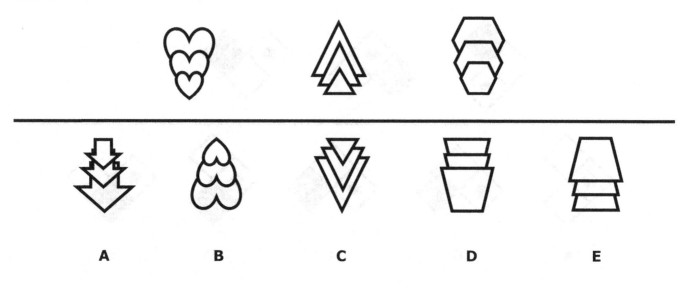

A   B   C   D   E

18.

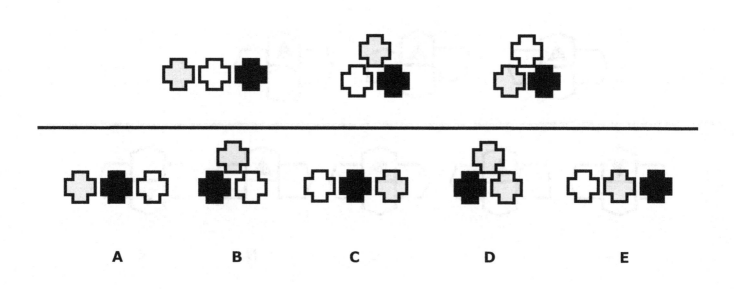

A   B   C   D   E

19.

20.

21.

22.

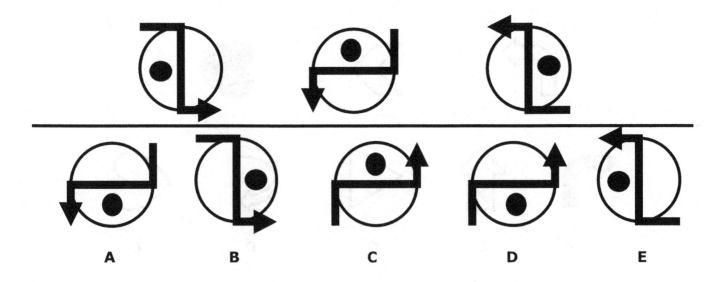

Paper Folding

Students need to determine the appearance of a perforated and folded sheet of paper, once opened.

Example

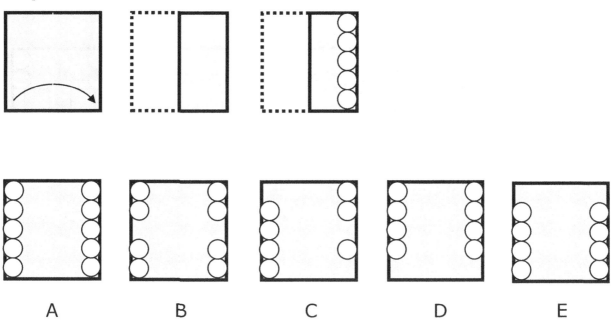

The figures at the top represent a square piece of paper being folded, and the last of these figures has 5 holes on it.

One of the lower five figures shows where the perforations will be when the paper is fully unfolded. You have to understand which of these images is the right one.

First, the paper was folded horizontally, from left to right.

Then, 5 holes was punched out. Therefore, when the paper is unfolded the holes will mirror on the left and right side of the sheet. The right answer is "A".

Tips for Paper Folding

The best way to get ready for these challenging questions is to practice. The patterns that show up on the test can confuse students, so the demonstration of folding and unfolding real paper can be very helpful.

1.

2.

3.

4.

5.

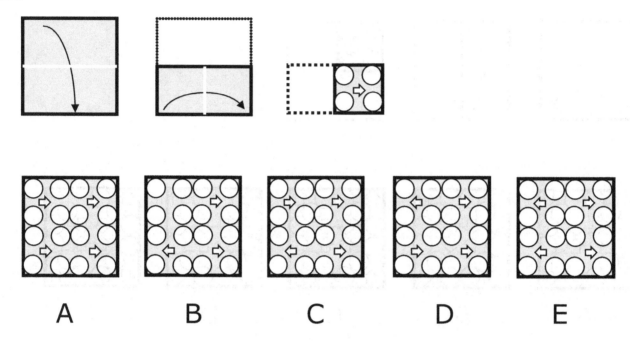

A B C D E

6.

A B C D E

7.

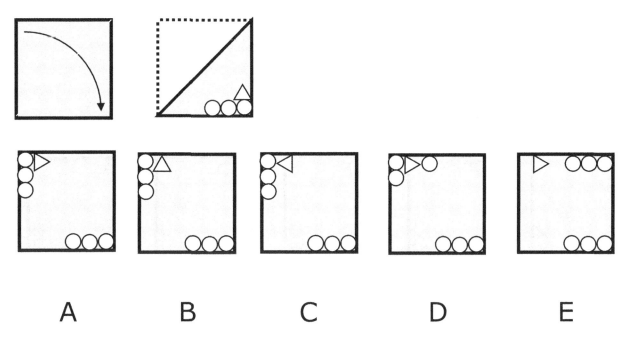

A   B   C   D   E

8.

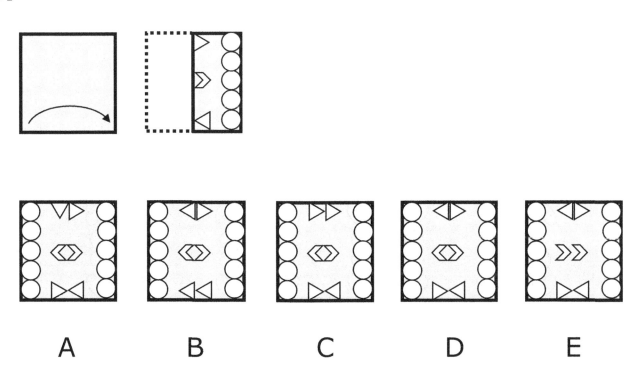

A   B   C   D   E

9.

10.

11.

12.

13.

14.

15.

16.

QUANTITATIVE BATTERY GRADE 6

This section introduces abstract reasoning and problem-solving skills to learners and is one of the most challenging sections in the test.

Number Puzzle

Students are required to solve basic mathematical equations. An equation says that two things are equal. It will have an equals sign "=" like this:

$$7 + 2 = 10 - 1$$

The equation says that what is on the left (7 + 2) is equal to what is on the right (10 − 1).

Example 1

$$? - 12 = 2$$

A 10   B 14   C 1   D 7   E 16

- The right side of the equal sign is 2. Which answer should be given in place of the question mark, so that the left side of the equal is also 2?
$$14 - 12 = 2; 2 = 2$$

The right answer is "B".

Example 2

$$? + \blacklozenge = 8$$

$$\blacklozenge = 1$$

A 1   B 13   C 7   D 8   E 9

? + 1= 8; 7+1=8; 8=8; the right answer is "C".

Tips for Number Puzzle

- Deeply understand the meaning of "equal", as the purpose is to provide the missing information that will make the two parts of the equation the same.
- Train yourself to solve simple basic equations.
- Practice with numbers and problem solving.

1.

$$? - 20 = 80$$

A 200   **B** 100   **C** 140   **D** 70   **E** 160

2.

$$? + \blacklozenge = 97$$

$$\blacklozenge = 86$$

A 11   **B** 13   **C** 50   **D** 18   **E** 19

3.

$$? + 22 = \blacklozenge$$

$$\blacklozenge = 318$$

A 221   **B** 296   **C** 110   **D** 298   **E** 220

4.

$$? \times 14 = \blacklozenge + 122$$

$$\blacklozenge = 4$$

A 10   **B** 9   **C** 8   **D** 4   **E** 12

5.

$$? - 3 = \blacklozenge + 8$$

$$\blacklozenge = 190$$

A 201   **B** 100   **C** 203   **D** 120   **E** 123

6.

$$121 + 13 = 560 - ?$$

A 422   **B** 426   **C** 301   **D** 601   **E** 10

7.

$$432 = 980 - 4 - ?$$

A 55   **B** 201   **C** 444   **D** 820   **E** 544

8.

$$401 = 600 - 201 + ?$$

A 120   **B** 4   **C** 100   **D** 6   **E** 2

9. $$1010 = 100 + 10 + ?$$

A 399   **B** 910   **C** 240   **D** 900   **E** 110

10.

$$770 - 21 = 890 - ?$$

A 220   **B** 200   **C** 141   **D** 360   **E** 190

11.

$$110 + 118 = 300 - ?$$

A 120   **B** 66   **C** 22   **D** 72   **E** 79

12.

$$76 : 4 = 65 - ?$$

A 49   **B** 46   **C** 26   **D** 36   **E** 15

13.

$$? = \blacklozenge : 3$$

$$\blacklozenge = 99$$

A 29   **B** 30   **C** 34   **D** 55   **E** 33

14.

$$? = \blacklozenge \times 22$$

$$\blacklozenge = 9$$

A 100   **B** 197   **C** 199   **D** 198   **E** 310

15.

$$? = \blacklozenge \times 240$$

$$\blacklozenge = 3$$

A 720   **B** 360   **C** 370   **D** 502   **E** 719

16.

$$? = \blacklozenge + 7$$

$$21 = \blacklozenge - \bullet$$

$$\bullet = 95$$

A 520   **B** 180   **C** 123   **D** 114   **E** 18

Number Analogies

In this session, you will see two pairs of numbers and then a number without its pair. The first two pairs of numbers are correlated in some way. Try to find out the correlation between the numbers within each of the pairs. Choose an answer that gives you the third pair of numbers, related to each other in the same way.

Example

[1 → 55]   [5 → 59]   [15 → ?]

A 78   **B** 180   **C** 69   **D** 70   **E** 12

- In the first two sets, you have 1 and 55; 5 and 59. Both numbers (1 and 5), increase by 54 (1+54=55; 5+54=59).
- Apply the same rule to the number 15.

15 + 54 = 69. The right answer is "C".

Tips for Number Analogies

- Step 1: acquire all the information from the two given pairs (relationships, sums, subtractions, etc.).
- Step 2: apply the same rules, relations, formulas that you correctly identified in step 1.
- Step 3: double-check that the rule has been properly applied.

1.

[80 → 102]   [55 → 77]   [99 → ?]

A 220   **B** 37   **C** 180   **D** 190   **E** 121

2.

[120 → 40]   [9 → 3]   [450 → ?]

A 90   **B** 10   **C** 150   **D** 98   **E** 110

3.

[560 → 499]   [100 → 39]   [69 → ?]

A 50   **B** 19   **C** 10   **D** 8   **E** 9

4.

[150 → 75]   [84 → 42]   [102 → ?]

A 45   **B** 11   **C** 51   **D** 120   **E** 22

5.

[80 → 16]   [95 → 19]   [35 → ?]

A 10   **B** 6   **C** 12   **D 7**   **E** 8

6.

[55 → 165]   [42 → 126]   [33 → ?]

A 270   **B** 110   **C** 14   **D** 99   **E** 97

7.

[42 → 6]   [77 → 11]   [777 → ?]

A 111   **B** 177   **C** 334   **D** 119   **E** 121

8.

[200 → 189]   [150 → 139]   [15 → ?]

A 1   **B** 2   **C** 4   **D** 60   **E** 8

9.

[65 ➝ 195]   [32 ➝ 96]   [12 ➝ ?]

A 31   **B** 36   **C** 30   **D** 21   **E** 28

10.

[256 ➝ 252]   [113 ➝ 109]   [78 ➝ ?]

A 74   **B** 78   **C** 39   **D** 90   **E** 8

11.

[20 ➝ 57]   [35 ➝ 102]   [12 ➝ ?]

A 10   **B** 11   **C** 33   **D** 29   **E** 20

12.

[84 ➝ 21]   [96 ➝ 24]   [100 ➝ ?]

A 52   **B** 14   **C** 30   **D** 21   **E** 25

13.

[192 → 24]   [360 → 45]   [96 → ?]

A 11   **B** 10   **C** 12   **D** 10   **E** 13

14.

[200 → 110]   [30 → 25]   [8 → ?]

A 20   **B** 44   **C** 10   **D** 21   **E** 14

15.

[1000 → 202]   [60 → 14]   [95 → ?]

A 50   **B** 22   **C** 21   **D** 20   **E** 34

16.

[484 → 284]   [652 → 452]   [282 → ?]

A 12   **B** 72   **C** 32   **D** 82   **E** 22

17.
[69 → 207]   [31 → 93]   [52 → ?]

A 110   **B** 156   **C** 130   **D** 131   **E** 290

18.
[310 → 156]   [44 → 23]   [8 → ?]

A 1   **B** 4   **C** 3   **D** 25   **E** 5

Number Series

Students are provided with a sequence of numbers that follow a pattern. They are required to identify which number should come next in the sequence.

Example 1

$$5 \quad 8 \quad 11 \quad 14 \quad ?$$

A 13   **B** 12   **C** 11   **D** 7   **E** 17

- It's easy to realize that each number in the sequence increases by 3. 5+3=8; 8+3=11; 11+3=14; etc.
- Apply the same rule to the number 14.

14 + 3 = 17. The right answer is "E".

Example 2

$$2 \quad 5 \quad 4 \quad 7 \quad 6 \quad ?$$

A 3   **B** 10   **C** 11   **D** 9   **E** 12

- The sequence follows the rule: +3, -1, +3, -1 etc. 2+3=5; 5-1=4; 4+3=7; 7-1=6; etc.
- Apply the same rule to the number 6.

6 + 3 = 9. The right answer is "D".

Tips for Number Series

- To correctly answer these questions, the student will need to be able to identify the patterns in a sequence of numbers and provide the missing item. Therefore, it is important to practice, working with sequences of numbers.

1.

      88   **61**   **82**   **55**   **?**

A 84   **B** 77   **C** 102   **D** 88   **E** 76

2.

      145   **139**   **174**   **168**   **203**   **?**

A 8   **B** 110   **C** 197   **D** 120   **E** 100

3.

      400   **407**   **362**   **369**   **324**   **?**

A 110   **B** 331   **C** 350   **D** 360   **E** 320

4.

    110 **105** **115** **109** **104** **114** **108 ?**

A 101   **B** 104   **C** 115   **D** 103   **E** 170

5.

1001   951   971   921   ?

A 941   **B** 790   **C** 890   **D** 901   **E** 860

6.

15   0   49   34   83   68   ?

A 200   **B** 40   **C** 117   **D** 115   **E** 92

7.

301   271   301   271   301
?

A 270   **B** 271   **C** 301   **D** 501   **E** 31

8.

9   27   18   36   27   45   ?

A 45   **B** 9   **C** 27   **D** 36   **E** 18

9.

666   599   602   535   538   ?

A 471   **B** 530   **C** 540   **D** 450   **E** 620

10.

221   270   260   309   299   348   ?

A 383   **B** 338   **C** 240   **D** 390   **E** 310

11.

701   720   700   719   699   718   ?

A 920   **B** 910   **C** 681   **D** 683   **E** 698

12.

334   274   286   226   238   178   ?

A 191   **B** 100   **C** 190   **D** 121   **E** 110

13.

      412   399   413   400   414   401   ?

A 412   **B** 415   **C** 200   **D** 451   **E** 120

14.

      0.04   0.13   0.11   0,2   0,18   0,27 ?

A 0.25   **B** 0.9   **C** 0.12   **D** 1   **E** 0.01

15.

      0.9   0.87   0.91   0.88   ?

A 0.90   **B** 0.95   **C** 0.35   **D** 0.92   **E** 0.1

16.

      67   134   66   133   65   ?

A 129   **B** 124   **C** 136   **D** 152   **E** 132

17.

1.5   5   4   7,5   6.5   10   ?

A 9   **B** 12,5   **C** 11,5   **D** 17.5   **E** 3,5

18.

44   22   34   12   24   2   ?

A 1   **B** 10.5   **C** 14   **D** 13   **E** 10

90

ANSWER KEY GRADE 6

Verbal Analogies Practice Test
p.19

1.
Answer: option A
Explanation: sorrow causes crying as happiness causes laughing.

2.
Answer: option B
Explanation: the answer is amend because that is the word formed by adding an "a" in front of mend.

3.
Answer: option C
Explanation: this is an analogy of degrees. Warm is less intense than hot, amusing is less intense than hilarious.

4.
Answer: option C
Explanation: a crumb is a very small piece that breaks off from a piece of bread. Splinter is a very small piece that breaks off from a piece of wood.

5.
Answer: option E
Explanation: an album is a place for saving photographs; a shelf is a place for saving books.

6.
Answer: option A
Explanation: a recipe is found in a cookbook; a map is found in an atlas.

7.
Answer: option C
Explanation: football is a sport; biology is a science.

8.

Answer: option D

Explanation: anonymous describes the lack of a name; formless describes the lack of shape.

9.

Answer: option A

Explanation: hand is a part of a man; paw is a part of a dog.

10.

Answer: option C

Explanation: an aspirin may cure a headache; an antibiotic may cure an infection.

11.

Answer: option C

Explanation: the words in each pair are antonyms.

12.

Answer: option E

Explanation: a troupe is a group of actors; a club is a group of members.

13.

Answer: option C

Explanation: Moon is a satellite; Earth is a planet.

14.

Answer: option A

Explanation: a forecast concerns a future event; a regret concerns a past event.

15.
Answer: option B
Explanation: a virus causes influenza; typhoid is caused by a bacterium.

16.
Answer: option E
Explanation: thermometer measures temperature; clock measures time.

17.
Answer: option B
Explanation: scribbling is an improper form of writing; stuttering is an improper form of speaking.

18.
Answer: option C
Explanation: the car is parked in the garage; the airplane is parked in the hangar.

19.
Answer: option A
Explanation: second is the place for performing the first.

20.
Answer: option B
Explanation: second is the path traced by the first.

21.
Answer: option E
Explanation: asylum represents a refuge, dungeon a confinement.

22.
Answer: option D

Explanation: second indicates the function performed by the first.

23.
Answer: option A

Explanation: the words in each pair are antonyms.

24.
Answer: option C

Explanation: poodle is a breed of dog; moose is a breed of deer.

Verbal Classification Practice Test
p.26

1.
Answer: option A
Explanation: two vowels each.

2.
Answer: option E
Explanation: clove, cinnamon, pepper and oregano are spices.

3.
Answer: option E
Explanation: zinc, iron, copper and aluminum are metals.

4.
Answer: option A
Explanation: parsley, basil, dill and oregano are types of herbs.

5.
Answer: option C
Explanation: clams, oysters, scallops and mussels are mollusks.

6.
Answer: option B
Explanation: snake, duck, tortoise and shark lay eggs.

7.
Answer: option C
Explanation: eyes, kidneys, ears and lungs are present in a pair in the human body.

8.
Answer: option B
Explanation: arc, diameter, radius and chord are related to circle.

9.
Answer: option E
Explanation: rose, lotus, marigold and tulip are type of flowers.

10.
Answer: option C
Explanation: duck, crocodile, frog and pelican can live in water habitat.

11.
Answer: option D
Explanation: coffee, milk, tea and water are liquids.

12.
Answer: option C
Explanation: curd, butter, cheese and cream are products obtained from milk.

13.
Answer: option B
Explanation: fingers, palm, thumb and phalanges are parts of hand.

14.
Answer: option E
Explanation: polyester, terylene, nylon and spandex are synthetic fibers.

15.
Answer: option B
Explanation: microscope, telescope, periscope and camera can be used with the eyes.

16.
Answer: option C
Explanation: cry, sob, weep and moan indicate a sad state of mind.

17.
Answer: option E
Explanation: medium, average, mediocre, intermediate are synonyms.

18.
Answer: option B
Explanation: honest, intelligent, wise and generous denote good qualities.

19.
Answer: option C
Explanation: basket, purse, bag, backpack are used to contain something.

20.
Answer: option D
Explanation: raid, attack, ambush and assault are forms of attack.
.

Sentence Completion Practice Test
p.32

1.
Answer: option A
Explanation: panic= a sudden strong feeling of fear or nervousness that makes you unable to think clearly or behave sensibly.

2.
Answer: option C
Explanation: shape= the form that something has.

3.
Answer: option A
Explanation: calculate= quantify how serious or effective it is.

4.
Answer: option B
Explanation: qualified= having suitable knowledge, experience, or skills, especially for a particular job.

5.
Answer: option C
Explanation: knowledge = the information, skills, and understanding that you have gained through learning or experience.

6.
Answer: option A
Explanation: waiting= the action of delaying action until a particular time or event.

7.
Answer: option B
Explanation: publish=to make official information such as a report available for everyone to read.

8.
Answer: option E
Explanation: announce = to officially tell people about something, especially about a plan or a decision.

9.
Answer: option B
Explanation: necessary = something that is necessary is what you need to have or need to do.

10.
Answer: option C
Explanation: nobody= no one.

11.
Answer: option D
Explanation: depressed = very unhappy

12.
Answer: option A
Explanation: conceive= to imagine a particular situation or to think about something in a particular way.

13.
Answer: option C
Explanation: warming = an increase in the temperature of something.

14.
Answer: option C
Explanation: depend= to need something or someone in order to exist.

15.
Answer: option D
Explanation: understand=to know or realize how a fact, process, situation etc. works, especially through learning or experience

16.
Answer: option D
Explanation: talent = a natural ability to do something well.

17.
Answer: option A
Explanation: other: used to refer to all things in a group apart from the one you have already mentioned.

18.
Answer: option D
Explanation: risk = an action that might have bad results.

19.
Answer: option B
Explanation: lead = to cause something to happen.

20.
Answer: option B
Explanation: economize = to reduce the amount of money, that you use.

Figure Matrices Practice Test
p.41

1.
Answer: option E
Explanation: the 4 black dots are removed.

2.
Answer: option B
Explanation: the circle in the upper right corner is removed.

3.
Answer: option C
Explanation: the two inside shapes are removed.

4.
Answer: option C
Explanation: the smaller figure moves into the center of the larger figure.

5.
Answer: option B
Explanation: windows addition to the figures on the left.

6.
Answer: option D
Explanation: addition of a vertical segment to the left figure.

7.
Answer: option A
Explanation: the 2 bottom petals shift 1 unit to the right and 1 unit to the left. The upper petal doesn't move.

8.
Answer: option C
Explanation: the opposite sector to the one of the figure on the left is colored.

9.
Answer: option D
Explanation: 90-degree clockwise rotation and the figure becomes black.

10.
Answer: option C
Explanation: the head becomes a square; the body becomes white.

11.
Answer: option E
Explanation: only the arms change direction and point upwards.

12.
Answer: option D
Explanation: the head becomes round.

13.
Answer: option B
Explanation: weights become triangular.

14.
Answer: option B
Explanation: the square becomes gray; 2 white circles are removed.

15.

Answer: option A

Explanation: the diagonals are eliminated. The figure becomes black with a gray heart in the center.

16.

Answer: option D

Explanation: the figure on the left doubles horizontally.

17.

Answer: option E

Explanation: the 2 black shapes become white and move in opposite position.

18.

Answer: option E

Explanation: the white triangle disappears. The gray circles turn white and move to the right.

19.

Answer: option A

Explanation: the bottom shape disappears; the top shape is placed inside the middle shape.

20.

Answer: option E

Explanation: the 2 shapes swap positions; the shape that was inside remains white; the gray shape changes color.

21.

Answer: option D

Explanation: the figure rotates by 90 degrees anticlockwise.

22.

Answer: option B

Explanation: the square at the top does not change. In the bottom square, there is the addition of 2 circles.

Figure Classification Practice Test
p.50

1.
Answer: option E.
Explanation: 2 concentric figures; inside figures are white; larger figures are black.

2.
Answer: option B
Explanation: same white rotated figure.

3.
Answer: option D
Explanation: a black star, a grey star and a black circle.

4.
Answer: option D
Explanation: combos of a cross, a heart pointing down and an arrow pointing right.

5.
Answer: option A
Explanation: combos of 2 white squares, a grey square and a black square. The 2 white squares are always side by side.

6.
Answer: option C
Explanation: same figure, rotated.

7.
Answer: option D
Explanation: combos of a white heart pointing up, a black heart pointing down, a grey heart pointing down, a white triangle pointing up.

8.
Answer: option A
Explanation: same grey figure, rotated.

9.
Answer: option C
Explanation: combos of a white triangle pointing up, a black triangle pointing down, a black triangle pointing up, a grey arrow pointing down.

10.
Answer: option C
Explanation: 2 arrow pointing right, 1 arrow pointing left.

11.
Answer: option E
Explanation: combos of 2 black circles, a gray circle and a white heart. The gray circle is always inside the white heart.

12.
Answer: option A
Explanation: 1 heart pointing down with a black dot, 1 triangle pointing up with a black dot, 1 white cross, 1 white triangle pointing down,

13.
Answer: option C
Explanation: 2 grey crosses, 1 black cross and 1 white cross. One of the 2 gray crosses is always placed to the right of all the others.

14.
Answer: option A

Explanation: each figure is made up of 2 equal shapes; the bottom one is the same as the top one but is flipped vertically.

15.
Answer: option C

Explanation: 1 black square, 1 gray square and 1 white square. The white square contains a black circle.

16.
Answer: option B

Explanation: each image consists of 4 equal shapes, some rotated differently. One of the shapes contains a black triangle pointing upwards and it is always placed in the same position.

17.
Answer: option E

Explanation: 3 same-type shapes, increasing size, from bottom to top.

18.
Answer: option E

Explanation: each image consists of 1 black cross, 1 gray cross and 1 white cross. The black cross is always placed in the lower right corner.

19.
Answer: option A

Explanation: each image consists of 4 squares, 2 gray and 2 white. All squares contain a black circle except one of gray squares.

20.
Answer: option D

Explanation: shapes pointing right.

21.

Answer: option A

Explanation: each image consists of 2 equal shapes, one gray and one white; the gray shape contains a black circle.

22.

Answer: option D

Explanation: same figure, rotated.

Paper Folding Practice Test
p.62

1.
Answer: option E

2.
Answer: option D

3.
Answer: option D

4.
Answer: option A

5.
Answer: option E

6.
Answer: option C

7
Answer: option A

8.
Answer: option D

9.
Answer: option B

10.
Answer: option D

11.
Answer: option A

12.
Answer: option E

13.
Answer: option D

14.
Answer: option B

15.
Answer: option C

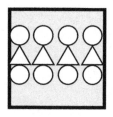

16.
Answer: option B

Number Puzzle Practice Test
p.73

1.
Answer: option B
Explanation: 100-20=80; 80=80

2.
Answer: option A
Explanation: 11+86=97; 97=97

3.
Answer: option B
Explanation: 296+22=318; 318=318

4.
Answer: option B
Explanation: 9X14=4+122; 126=126

5.
Answer: option A
Explanation: 201-3=190+8; 198=198

6.
Answer: option B
Explanation: 121+13=560-426; 134=134

7.
Answer: option E
Explanation: 432=980-4-544; 432=432

8.
Answer: option E
Explanation: 401=600-201+2; 401=399+2; 401=401

9.
Answer: option D
Explanation: 1010=100+10+900; 1010=110+900; 1010=1010

10.
Answer: option C
Explanation: 770-21=890-141; 749=749

11.
Answer: option D
Explanation: 110+118=300-72; 228=228

12.
Answer: option B
Explanation: 76: 4 =65-46; 19=19

13.
Answer: option E
Explanation: 33=99:3; 33=33

14.
Answer: option D
Explanation: 198=9X22; 198=198

15.
Answer: option A
Explanation: 720=3X240; 720=720

16.
Answer: option C
Explanation: $\blacklozenge$ = 21+95; $\blacklozenge$ =116; 123=116+7

Number Analogies Practice Test
p.79

1.
Answer: option E
Explanation: 80+22=102   56+22=77   99+22=121

2.
Answer: option C
Explanation: 120:3=40   9:3=3   450:3=150

3.
Answer: option D
Explanation: 560-61=499   100-61=39   69-61=8

4.
Answer: option C
Explanation: 150:2=75   84:2=42   102:2=51

5.
Answer: option D
Explanation: 80:5=16   95:5=19   35:5=7

6.
Answer: option D
Explanation: 55X3=165   42X3=126   33X3=99

7.
Answer: option A
Explanation: 42:7=6   77:7=11   777:7=111

8.
Answer: option C
Explanation: 200-11=189   150-11=139   15-11=4

9.
Answer: option B
Explanation: 65X3=195   32X3=96   12X3=36

10.
Answer: option A
Explanation: 256-4=252   113-4=109   78-4=74

11.
Answer: option C
Explanation: 20X3=60; 60-3=57   35X3=105; 105-3=102   12X3=36; 36-3=33

12.
Answer: option E
Explanation: 84:4=21   96:4=24   100:4=25

13.
Answer: option C
Explanation: 192:8=24   360:8=45   96:8=12

14.
Answer: option E
Explanation: 200:2=100; 100+10=110   30:2=15; 15+10=25   8:2=4 4+10=14

15.
Answer: option C
Explanation: 1000:5=200; 200+2=202   60:5=12; 12+2=14 95:5=19; 19+2=21

16.
Answer: option D
Explanation: 484-200=284   652-200=452   282-200=82

17.
Answer: option B
Explanation: 69X3=207   31X3=93   52X3=156

18.
Answer: option E
Explanation: 310:2=155; 155+1=156   44:2=22; 22+1=23
8:2=4; 4+1=5

Number Series Practice Test
p.85

1.
Answer: option E
Explanation: -27, +21, -27, +21 etc.

2.
Answer: option C
Explanation: -6, +35, -6, +35, -6, etc.

3.
Answer: option B
Explanation: +7, -45, +7, -45, +7, etc.

4.
Answer: option D
Explanation: -5, +10, -6, -5, +10, -6, -5, etc.

5.
Answer: option A
Explanation: -50, +20, -50, +20, etc.

6.
Answer: option C
Explanation: -15, +49, -15, +49, -15, +49, etc.

7.
Answer: option B
Explanation: -30, +30, -30, +30, -30, etc.

8.
Answer: option D
Explanation: +18, -9, +18, -9, +18, -9, etc.

9.
Answer: option A
Explanation: -67, +3, -67, +3, -67, etc.

10.
Answer: option B
Explanation: +49, -10, +49, -10, +49, -10, etc.

11.
Answer: option E
Explanation: +19, -20, +19, -20, +19, -20, etc.

12.
Answer: option C
Explanation: -60, +12, -60, +12, -60, +12, etc.

13.
Answer: option B
Explanation: -13, +14, -13, +14, -13, +14, etc.

14.
Answer: option A
Explanation: +0.09, -0.02, +0.09, -0.02, +0.09, -0.02, etc.

15.
Answer: option D
Explanation: -0.03, +0.04, -0.03, +0.04, etc.

16.
Answer: option E
Explanation: +67, -68, +67, -68, +67, -68, etc.

17.
Answer: option A
Explanation: +3.5, -1, +3.5, -1, +3.5, -1, etc.

18.
Answer: option C
Explanation: -22, +12, -22, +12, -22, +12, etc.

HOW TO DOWNLOAD 54 BONUS QUESTIONS

Thank you for reading this book, we hope you really enjoyed it and found it very helpful.

PLEASE LEAVE US A REVIEW ON THE WEBSITE WHERE YOU PURCHASED THIS BOOK!

By leaving a review, you give us the opportunity to improve our work.

A GIFT FOR YOU!

FREE ONLINE ACCESS TO 54 BONUS PRACTICE QUESTIONS.

Follow this link:

https://www.skilledchildren.com/free-download-cogat-grade-6-test-prep.php

You will find a PDF to download: please insert this PASSWORD: 556667

Nicole Howard and the SkilledChildren.com Team

www.skilledchildren.com

COGAT® TEST PREP
GRADE 7/8

VERBAL BATTERY GRADE 7/8

This section is designed to assess a student's vocabulary, ability to solve problems associated with vocabulary, ability to determine word relationship and memory retention.

Verbal Analogies

A verbal analogy traces a similarity between a pair of words and another pair of words.

Example

napoleon → baker : pergola →

A carpenter   **B** general   **C** mammal   **D** plumber   **E** teacher

- First, identify the relationship between the first pair of words.
- How do the words "napoleon" and "baker" go together?

A napoleon is a pastry made by a baker.

- Now, look at the word "pergola".
- Which of the possible choices follows the previous rule?

A pergola is made by a carpenter, so the correct answer is A.

Tips for Solving Verbal Analogies

- Try to identify the correlation between the first two words.
- Review all answers before you make a choice.
- Remove any word in the answers that don't have a comparable kind of relationship.
- Also, evaluate the possible alternative meanings of the words.

1.

annoy → enrage : enlarge →

A increase   **B** reduce   **C** exaggerate
D   augment   **E** create

2.

tear → tr: near →

A fear   **B** nr   **C** ay   **D** new   **E** old

3.

smart → genius : cold →

A warm   **B** hot   **C** amusing   **D** impossible
E freezing

4.

chair → sit : car →

A drive   **B** wheel   **C** sofa   **D** lamp   **E** race

5.

sun →burn : fire →

A light   **B** dark   **C** smoke   **D** paper   **E** skin

6.

day → week : afternoon →

A time   **B** Monday   **C** sunrise   **D** morning
E month

7.

ornithology → birds : seismology →

A flowers   **B** earthquakes   **C** science   **D** dogs
E poems

8.

eat → ate : win →

A comb   **B** ated   **C** won   **D** winded   **E** wind

9.

broken → repair : itch →

A sleep **B** scratch **C** eat **D** fall **E** remember

10.

grain → grail : brain →

A head **B** brail **C** train **D** plant **E** wheat

11.

train → board : horse →

A mount **B** shoe **C** pick **D** stable **E** fall

12.

feta → Greek : mozzarella →

A salad **B** Italian **C** yellow **D** milk **E** French

13.

shoe ⟶ loafer: moccasin ⟶

A food **B** alligator **C** snake **D** asteroid **E** lizard

14.

Nord ⟶ Sud : composure ⟶

A past **B** joy **C** time D fear **E** Est

15.

mad ⟶ insane: stupid ⟶

A clever **B** obstinate **C** true **D** desperate
E obtuse

16.

lion ⟶ ion: loan ⟶

A cat **B** oan **C** ione **D** on **E** lione

17.

repair → damage : segregate →

A isolate **B** speak **C** push **D** damage **E** unify

18.

primate → monkey : marsupial →

A bear **B** opossum **C** dog **D** cat **E** gorilla

19.

singe → char: congeal →

A solidify **B** evaporate **C** resolve **D** conceal
E create

20.

flash → camera : mouse →

A track **B** cord **C** computer **D** street
E radio

21.

king → chess : shuttlecock →

A tennis **B** labyrinth **C** classroom **D** badminton.
E church

22.

forehand → tennis : swing →

A golf **B** score **C** racket **D** ski **E** ball

23.

inhale → sniff : lop →

A bite **B** close **C** snip **D** adhere **E** crush

24.

legume → bean : wheat →

A soup **B** carrot **C** barley **D** apple **E** spelt

Verbal Classification

Verbal classification questions ask the student to choose the voice that belongs to a group of three words.

Example

Venus, Earth, Mars

A Sun   **B** Italy   **C** extraterrestrial   **D** rock   **E** Mercury

- First, identify the relationship between the three words in the first row.
- What do the words Venus, Earth, and Mars have in common?

Venus, Mars and Earth are planets.

- Now, look at the five worlds: Sun, Italy, extraterrestrial, rock, Mercury. Which word goes best with the three words in the top row?

Mercury is also a planet, so the correct answer is E.

Tips for Solving Verbal Classification Questions

- Try to identify the correlation between the three words in the top row.
- Review all answers before you make a choice.
- Remove every word in the answers that don't have any kind of relationship with the three words in the top row.
- Also, evaluate the possible alternative meanings of the words.

1.

rose, nose, glucose

A microsecond.   **B** flower   **C** face   **D** cellulose
E sugar

2.

temperature, wind, humidity

A cloudiness   **B** sun   **C** rain   **D** fog
E mud

3.

Akita, Autralian Terrier, Barbet

A dog   **B** cat   **C** Basset Hound   **D** Abyssinian
E Birman

4.

Kimberlite, Pumice, Basalt

A Iron   **B** Aluminum   **C** Dacite   **D** Steel
E rock

5.

aspirin, paracetamol, ibuprofen

A coffee   **B** codeine   **C** ginger   **D** turmeric
E ginseng

6.

nuclear, thermal, chemical

A kinetic   **B** sturdy   **C** compact   **D** halogen
E colorful

7.

halogen, incandescent, led

A blinding   **B** dazzling   **C** fluorescent   **D** pale
E bright

8.

black, green, rooibos

A orange juice   **B** water   **C** coffee   **D** oolong
E lemonade

9.

artificial, glacial, saline

A metallic **B** polluted **C** volcanogenic **D** new
E nice

10.

igloo, apartment, cottage

A garden **B** wall **C** window **D** villa **E** door

11.

name, milk, baby

A gold **B** house **C** oxygen **D** rainbow **E** silver

12.

singular, plural, proper

A one **B** thing **C** concrete **D** crowd
E qualifying

13.
country, jazz, metal

A discordant   **B** unknown   **C** party   **D** funk
E fast

14.
small, class, press

A cotton   **B** meet   **C** week   **D** wood   **E** spell

15.
determiner, adverb, pronoun

A preposition   **B** some   **C** pronunciation   **D** wife
E parts

16.
passive, linking, transitive

A new **B** old **C** intransitive **D** action **E** combining

17.

saw, used, drove

A have   **B** wrote   **C** drive   **D** see   **E** driver

18.

combination, decomposition, combustion

A creation   **B** lighting   **C** death   **D** firing
E   neutralization

19.

femur, patella, tibia

A humerus   **B** ulna   **C** fibula   **D** sphenoid
E radius

20.

angiosperms, deciduous, evergreens

A greens   **B** gymnosperms   **C** beans   **D** timeless
E leaves

Sentence Completion

Complete the phrase using the appropriate word that best fits the meaning of the sentence as a whole.

Example

We are having spaghetti for dinner and apple dumpling for ....

A fun   **B** dessert   **C** loving   **D** drink   **E** toy

- First, read the sentence. You will realize that one word is missing.
- Look at the answer choices under the main sentence. Which word would go better in the phrase?

Apple= sweet tasting fruit that can be eaten as dessert. Therefore, the right choice is "B".

Tips for Sentence Completion

- First, read the incomplete phrase.
- Think about what type of word you can use and try to anticipate the answer.
- Remove every word in the answers that don't have any kind of relationship with the main sentence.
- Read the incomplete sentence again.

1.

He was a safe guy. He was decent, kind and _____, he put others before himself.

A stupid   **B** caring   **C** nice   **D** poor   **E** beautiful

2.

Britain and France _____ war on Germany in 1939 as a result of the invasion of Poland.

A declare   **B** refused   **C** declared   **D** ended
E left

3.

"Intricate" suggests such interlacing of parts as to make it nearly impossible to follow or _____ them separately.

A calculate   **B** construct   **C** spend   **D** buy
E grasp

4.

A war of nerves is a situation, often before a competition or battle, in which each opposing side _____ to frighten or discourage the other by making threats or by showing how strong it is.

A attempts   **B** escapes   **C** steals   **D** kills   **E** drink

5.

She must have _____ a dictionary, because it was very hard to follow along with all the big words she was throwing around.

A ordered   **B** sold   **C** swallowed   **D** loved   **E** burned

6.

The stomach is an organ in the body where food is digested, or the soft front part of your body just _____ the chest.

A above   **B** across   **C** behind   **D** below   **E** on

7.

You'd think he'd be wise as an owl after so many years in this industry, _____ he's still a careless old fool.

A and   **B** so   **C** indeed   **D** but   **E** therefore

8.

The owl was once a symbol of Athena, the Greek goddess of wisdom, and has endured as a symbol of _____ throughout the ages.

A wisdom   **B** strength   **C** love   **D** beauty
E eternity

9.

A pronoun is any member of a small class of words found in many languages that are used as _____ for nouns and noun phrases.

A verbs   **B** actions   **C** substitutes   **D** names
E words

10.

DNA determines the particular structure and functions of every _____ and is responsible for characteristics being passed on from parents to their children.

A children   **B** man   **C** cell   **D** head   **E** hand

11.

Tornado is a violent storm with strong winds that spin very quickly in a circle, often forming a cloud that is _____ at the bottom than the top.

A wider   **B** narrower   **C** drier   **D** higher   **E** fatter

12.

Ancient Greek political ideas, philosophy, art, architecture, literature, and science have had a _____ influence on how people in Europe live and think.

A nice   **B** bad   **C** great   **D** low   **E** secondary

13.

What the public and governments have to _____ is the need for nuclear energy versus the risk of another Chernobyl-type accident.

A assess   **B** watch   **C** hope   **D** prefer   **E** modify

14.

Collagen is a protein often used in beauty products and treatments to make people look younger and more _____.

A smarter   **B** attractive   **C** peaceful   **D** active
E relaxed

15.

A gas liquefies when the attractive forces between the molecules are sufficient to_____ them together in liquid form.

A burn   **B** separate   **C** bind   **D** vaporize
E detach

16.

Harry was plagued with one illness after another throughout his childhood, mainly suffering from asthma and other _____ problems.

A heart   **B** brain   **C** breathing   **D** mobility
E teeth

17.
Head-injured patients are normally admitted to hospital and _____ there until it is certain that they are fully fit to return home.

A tied   **B** jailed   **C** isolated   **D** kept   **E** cuffed

18.
The layer of ozone in the Earth's atmosphere, which blocks most _____ radiation, has become thinner in some places.

A acid   **B** colorful   **C** gamma   **D** infrared
E ultraviolet

19.

Some volcanoes produce only one kind of _____ during their entire lives, but others show an impressive diversity.

A fire   **B** water   **C** rock   **D** smoke   **E** gas

20.

The Earth orbits the Sun once a _____, and the Moon orbits the Earth approximately every 27 days.

A day   **B** month   **C** hour   **D** year   **E** week

NON VERBAL BATTERY GRADE 7/8

This section is designed to assess a student's ability to reason and think beyond what they've already been taught. This section includes geometric shapes and figures that aren't normally seen in the classroom.

Figure Matrices

Students are provided with a 2X2 matrix with the image missing in one cell. They have to identify the relationship between the two spatial shapes in the upper line and find a fourth image that has the same correlation with the left shape in the lower line.

Example

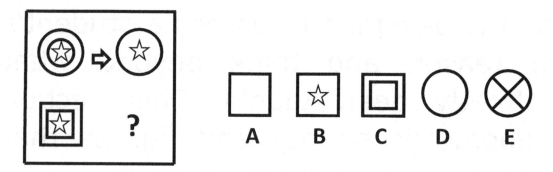

In the upper left box, the image shows a star inside 2 white concentric circles.
The upper right image shows only a star inside a white circle.
In the lower left box, the image shows a star inside 2 white concentric squares.
Which answer choice would go with this image in the same way as the upper images go together?

The image of the answer choice must show a star inside a white square. The right answer is "B".

Tips for Figure Matrices

- Consider all the answer choices before selecting one.
- Try to use logic and sequential reasoning.
- Eliminate the logically wrong answers to restrict the options.
- Train yourself to decipher the relationship between different figures and shapes.

1.

2.

3.

4.

5.

6.

7.

8.

9.

10.

11.

12.

13.

A   B   C   D   E

14.

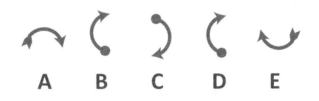

A   B   C   D   E

15.

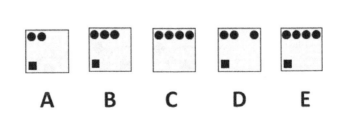

A   B   C   D   E

16.

17.

18.

19.

20.

21.

22.

Figure Classification

Students are provided with three shapes and they have to select the answer choice that should be the fourth figure in the set, based on the similarity with the other three figures. The intention is to test the student's ability to recognize similar patterns and to make a rational choice.

Example

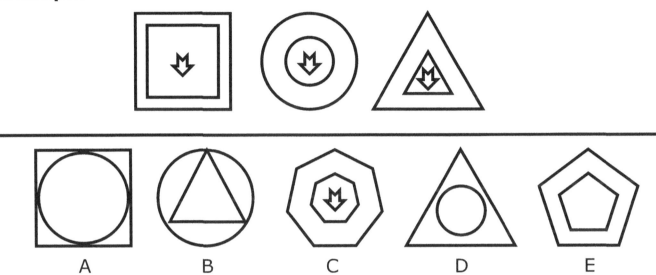

Look at the three pictures on the top. What do these three figures have in common?

You can see a white arrow in a square in a bigger square, a white arrow in a circle in a bigger circle, a white arrow in a triangle in a bigger triangle.

Now, look at the shapes in the row of the answer choices. Which image matches best the three shapes in the top row?

The image of the answer choice must show two identical figures, the smaller one inside the larger one and a white arrow inside the smaller one. The right answer is "C" (a smaller heptagon in a larger heptagon and a white arrow inside the smaller heptagon.)

Tips for Figure Classification

- Be sure to review all answer choices before selecting one.
- Try to use logic and sequential reasoning.
- Try to exclude the obviously wrong options to reduce the answer choices.

1.

2.

3.

4.

5.

A   **B**   **C**   **D**   **E**

6.

A   **B**   **C**   **D**   **E**

7.

A   **B**   **C**   **D**   **E**

8.

A   **B**   **C**   **D**   **E**

9.

A   **B**   **C**   **D**   **E**

10.

A   **B**   **C**   **D**   **E**

11.

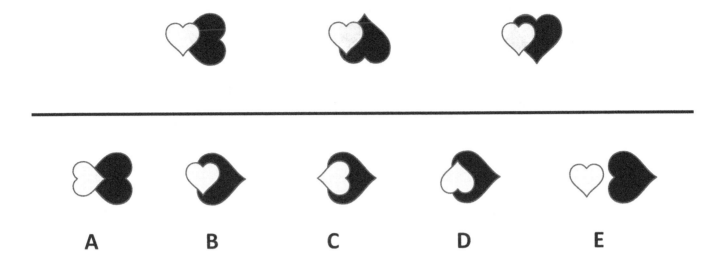

A   B   C   D   E

12.

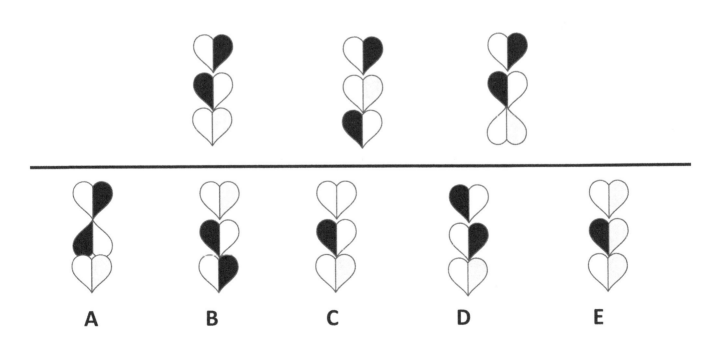

A   B   C   D   E

13.

14.

15.

16.

17.

A   **B**   **C**   **D**   **E**

18.

A   **B**   **C**   **D**   **E**

19.

20.

21.

22.

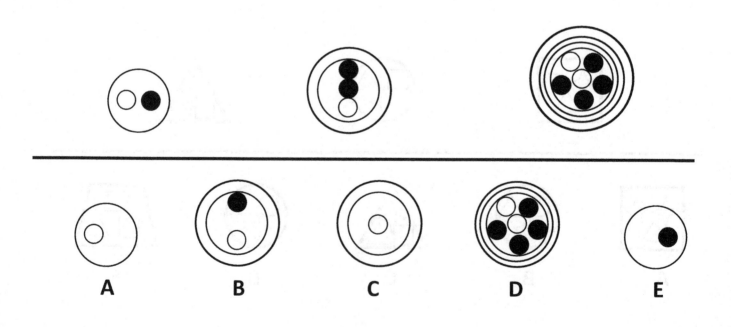

Paper Folding

Students need to determine the appearance of a perforated and folded sheet of paper, once opened.

Example

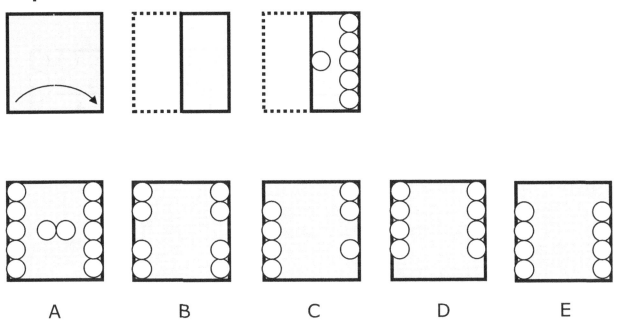

The figures at the top represent a square piece of paper being folded, and the last of these figures has 6 holes on it.

One of the lower five figures shows where the perforations will be when the paper is fully unfolded. You have to understand which of these images is the right one.

First, the paper was folded horizontally, from left to right.

Then, 6 holes was punched out. Therefore, when the paper is unfolded the holes will mirror on the left and right side of the sheet. The right answer is "A".

Tips for Paper Folding

The best way to get ready for these challenging questions is to practice. The patterns that show up on the test can confuse students, so the demonstration of folding and unfolding real paper can be very helpful.

1.

    A   B   C   D   E

2.

    A   B   C   D   E

3.

4.

5.

6.

7.

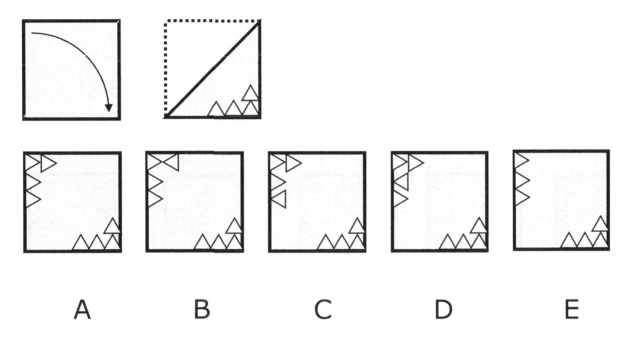

A   B   C   D   E

8.

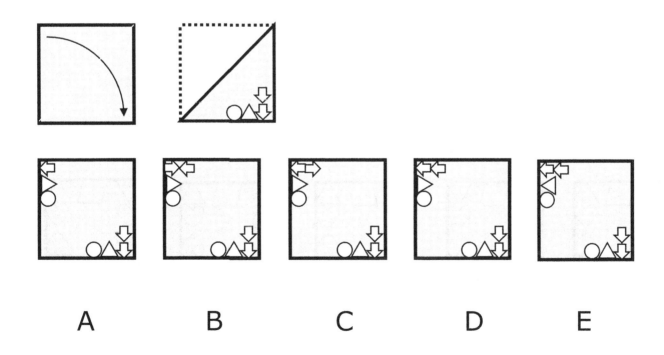

A   B   C   D   E

9.

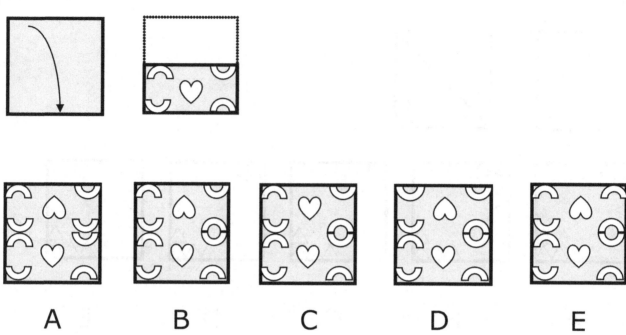

A   B   C   D   E

10.

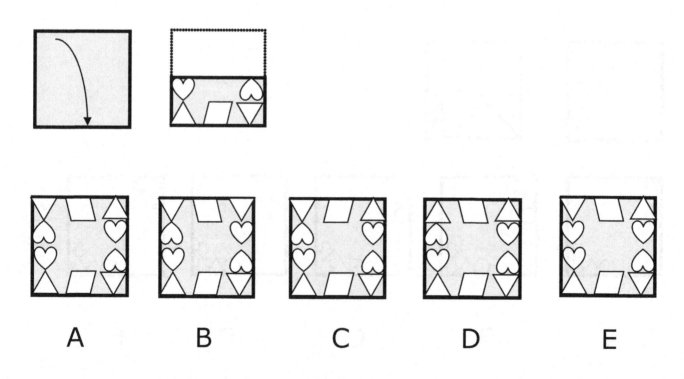

A   B   C   D   E

11.

12.

13.

14.

15.

16.

QUANTITATIVE BATTERY GRADE 7/8

This section introduces abstract reasoning and problem-solving skills to learners and is one of the most challenging sections in the test.

Number Puzzle

Students are required to solve basic mathematical equations. An equation says that two things are equal. It will have an equals sign "=" like this:

$$8 + 2 = 11 - 1$$

The equation says that what is on the left (8 + 2) is equal to what is on the right (11 − 1).

Example 1

$$? - 13 = 4$$

A 11   B 17   C 2   D 8   E 21

- The right side of the equal sign is 4. Which answer should be given in place of the question mark, so that the left side of the equal is also 4?

$$17 - 13 = 4; \; 4=4$$

The right answer is "B".

Example 2

$$? \; + \; \blacklozenge \; = 11$$

$$\blacklozenge = 3$$

A 12   **B** 14   **C** 8   **D** 7   **E** 5

? + 3= 11; 8+3=11; 11=11; the right answer is "C".

Tips for Number Puzzle

- Deeply understand the meaning of "equal", as the purpose is to provide the missing information that will make the two parts of the equation the same.
- Train yourself to solve simple basic equations. Practice with numbers and problem solving.

1.

$$? - 20 = 150$$

A 220 **B** 170 **C** 150 **D** 65 **E** 165

2.

$$? + \blacklozenge = 970$$

$$\blacklozenge = 860$$

A 110 **B** 130 **C** 501 **D** 118 **E** 119

3.

$$? + 212 = \blacklozenge$$

$$\blacklozenge = 3456$$

A 3244 **B** 29 **C** 15 **D** 2980 **E** 21

4.

$$? \times 21 = \blacklozenge - 436$$

$$\blacklozenge = 625$$

A 11   **B** 99   **C** 18   **D** 410   **E** 9

5.

$$? - 31 = \blacklozenge + 26$$

$$\blacklozenge = 945$$

A 2225   **B** 1002   **C** 203   **D** 112   **E** 145

6.

$$1123 + 131 = 5600 - ?$$

A 36   **B** 4110   **C** 4346   **D** 611   **E** 1

7.

$$4136 = 9110 - 45 - ?$$

A 155   **B** 20   **C** 4440   **D** 8200   **E** 4929

8.

$$7477 = 6000 - 211 + ?$$

A 1120   **B** 1400   **C** 10   **D** 1688   **E** 112

9. $$4012 = 1100 + 25 + ?$$

A 2887   **B** 91   **C** 1240   **D** 908   **E** 2100

10.

$$7170 - 33 = 8990 - ?$$

A 22   **B** 1853   **C** 1141   **D** 3360   **E** 1190

11.

$$99 + 1180 = 4000 - ?$$

A 1200   **B** 2721   **C** 220   **D** 7200   **E** 790

12.

$$1760 : 4 = 650 - ?$$

A 490   **B** 2500   **C** 210   **D** 6058   **E** 1500

13.

$$? = \blacklozenge : 3$$

$$\blacklozenge = 3900$$

A 129   **B** 300   **C** 1340   **D** 1300   **E** 3300

14.

$$? = \blacklozenge \times 15$$

$$\blacklozenge = 14$$

A 210   **B** 198   **C** 211   **D** 195   **E** 304

15.

$$? = \blacklozenge \times 24$$

$$\blacklozenge = 12$$

A 420   **B** 260   **C** 288   **D** 512   **E** 712

16.

$$? = \blacklozenge + 77$$

$$210 = \blacklozenge - \bullet$$

$$\bullet = 115$$

A 521   **B** 480   **C** 423   **D** 402   **E** 118

Number Analogies

In this session, you will see two pairs of numbers and then a number without its pair. The first two pairs of numbers are correlated in some way. Try to find out the correlation between the numbers within each of the pairs. Choose an answer that gives you the third pair of numbers, related to each other in the same way.

Example

[1 → 66]   [5 → 70]   [15 → ?]

A 75   **B** 170   **C** 80   **D** 72   **E** 122

- In the first two sets, you have 1 and 66; 5 and 70. Both numbers (1 and 5), increase by 65 (1+65=66; 5+65=70).
- Apply the same rule to the number 15.

15 + 65 = 80. The right answer is "C".

Tips for Number Analogies

- Step 1: acquire all the information from the two given pairs (relationships, sums, subtractions, etc.).
- Step 2: apply the same rules, relations, formulas that you correctly identified in step 1.
- Step 3: double-check that the rule has been properly applied.

1.

[72 → 1472]   [5 → 1405]   [9 → ?]

A 21   **B** 370   **C** 166   **D** 1900   **E** 1409

2.

[1250 → 250]   [625 → 125]   [35550 → ?]

A 7110   **B** 100   **C** 1500   **D** 9800   **E** 7500

3.

[5160 → 5101]   [125 → 66]   [619 → ?]

A 501   **B** 560   **C** 101   **D** 801   **E** 99

4.

[1569 → 523]   [126 → 42]   [729 → ?]

A 415   **B** 311   **C** 153   **D** 120   **E** 243

5.

[805 → 161]   [950 → 190]   [355→?]

A 101   **B** 16   **C** 112   **D** 71   **E** 85

6.

[93 → 465]   [41→ 205]   [27 → ?]

A 271   **B** 135   **C** 114   **D** 906   **E** 197

7.

[42 → 6]   [77 → 11]   [777 → ?]

A 111   **B** 177   **C** 334   **D** 119   **E** 121

8.

[4280 → 535]   [1888 →236]   [384 → ?]

A 48   **B** 288   **C** 48   **D** 608   **E** 18

9.

[15 → 37.5]   [8 → 20]   [11 → ?]

A 21   **B** 36.5   **C** 27.5   **D** 2.5   **E** 29.5

10.

[224 → 211]   [1131 → 1118]   [129 → ?]

A 174   **B** 718   **C** 139   **D** 116   **E** 80

11.

[17 → 64]   [31 → 120]   [13 → ?]

A 11   **B** 110   **C** 48   **D** 290   **E** 21

12.

[108 → 18]   [84 → 14]   [144 → ?]

A 24   **B** 18   **C** 31   **D** 121   **E** 22

13.

[315 → 90]   [28 → 8]   [56 → ?]

A 16   **B** 40   **C** 19   **D** 20   **E** 21

14.

[200 → 110]   [30 → 25]   [8 → ?]

A 17   **B** 18   **C** 2   **D** 22   **E** 14

15.

[1000 → 250]   [396 → 99]   [220 → ?]

A 50   **B** 122   **C** 210   **D** 55   **E** 58

16.

[600 → 210]   [417 → 149]   [918 → ?]

A 120   **B** 172   **C** 316   **D** 820   **E** 122

17.

[225 → 15]   [240 → 16]   [375 → ?]

A 11   **B** 25   **C** 113   **D** 13   **E** 29

18.

[4 → 396]   [7 → 693]   [8 → ?]

A 184   **B** 741   **C** 133   **D** 250   **E** 792

Number Series

Students are provided with a sequence of numbers that follow a pattern. They are required to identify which number should come next in the sequence.

Example 1

$$6 \quad 11 \quad 16 \quad 21 \quad ?$$

A 20   **B** 13   **C** 12   **D** 17   **E** 26

- It's easy to realize that each number in the sequence increases by 5. 6+5=11; 11+5=16; 16+5=21; etc.
- Apply the same rule to the number 21.

21 + 5 = 26. The right answer is "E".

Example 2

$$1 \quad 4 \quad 3 \quad 6 \quad 5 \quad ?$$

A 3   **B** 10   **C** 11   **D** 8   **E** 12

- The sequence follows the rule: +3, -1, +3, -1 etc. 1+3=4; 4-1=3; 3+3=6; 6-1=5; etc.
- Apply the same rule to the number 5.

5 + 3 = 8. The right answer is "D".

Tips for Number Series

- To correctly answer these questions, the student will need to be able to identify the patterns in a sequence of numbers and provide the missing item. Therefore, it is important to practice, working with sequences of numbers.

1.

95   74   89   68   ?

A 81   **B** 83   **C** 105   **D** 98   **E** 71

2.

666   612   629   575   592   ?

A 18   **B** 510   **C** 538   **D** 520   **E** 500

3.

568   523   569   524   570   ?

A 510   **B** 506   **C** 555   **D** 525   **E** 321

4.

796 791 801 798 793 803 800 ?

A 795   **B** 704   **C** 715   **D** 703   **E** 770

5.

1567   **1164**   **1189**   **786**   **?**

A 942   **B** 890   **C** 811   **D** 801   **E** 1060

6.

115   **0**   **1**   **21**   **-94**   **-93**   **?**

A -100   **B** 45   **C** -17   **D** 73   **E** -73

7.

399   **340**   **383**   **324**   **367**   **?**

A 370   **B** 308   **C** 311   **D** 401   **E** 310

8.

99   **84**   **88**   **82**   **67**   **71**   **?**

A 65   **B** 96   **C** 25   **D** 38   **E** 19

9.

1662   1687   1651   1676   1640   ?

A 1471   **B** 1530   **C** 1665   **D** 455   **E** 1620

10.

126   141   135   152   167   161   ?

A 178   **B** 138   **C** 125   **D** 190   **E** 110

11.

950   927   939   916   928   905   ?

A 960   **B** 910   **C** 781   **D** 908   **E** 917

12.

1000   998   1013   1013   1011   1026 ?

A 1910   **B** 1026   **C** 1190   **D** 1121   **E** 1110

13.

458   433   431   425   400   398   ?

A 380   **B** 315   **C** 300   **D** 392   **E** 320

14.

0.09   0.15   0.11   0.17   0.13   0.19   ?

A 0.15   **B** 0.67   **C** 0.11   **D** 2   **E** 0.31

15.

0.45   0.33   0.83   0.71   ?

A 0.22   **B** 1.66   **C** 0.45   **D** 1.21   **E** 0.1

16.

166   99   101   34   36   ?

A -34   **B** -4   **C** 12   **D** -13   **E** -31

17.

95.5   101   99   104.5   102.5   ?

A 100   **B** 112.5   **C** 108   **D** 170.5   **E** 13.5

18.

312   211   236   135   160   59   ?

A 100   **B** 10   **C** 84   **D** 130   **E** 110

HOW TO DOWNLOAD 54 BONUS QUESTIONS

Thank you for reading this book, we hope you really enjoyed it and found it very helpful.

PLEASE LEAVE US A REVIEW ON THE WEBSITE WHERE YOU PURCHASED THIS BOOK!

By leaving a review, you give us the opportunity to improve our work.

A GIFT FOR YOU!

FREE ONLINE ACCESS TO 54 BONUS PRACTICE QUESTIONS.

Follow this link:

https://www.skilledchildren.com/free-download-cogat-grade-7-test-prep.php

You will find a PDF to download: please insert this PASSWORD: 660301

Nicole Howard and the SkilledChildren.com Team

www.skilledchildren.com

ANSWER KEY GRADE 7/8

Verbal Analogies Practice Test
p.127

1.
Answer: option C
Explanation: To enrage is to annoy, but to a greater degree. To exaggerate is to enlarge, but to a greater degree.

2.
Answer: option B
Explanation: the answer is nr because the first and last letter of the word form it.

3.
Answer: option E
Explanation: this is an analogy of degrees. Genius is more intense than smart, freezing is more intense than cold.

4.
Answer: option A
Explanation: the purpose of a chair is to sit. The purpose of a car is to drive.

5.
Answer: option C
Explanation: burn is an effect of sun; smoke is an effect of fire.

6.
Answer: option D
Explanation: sequence analogies.

7.
Answer: option B
Explanation: ornithology studies birds. Seismology studies earthquakes.

8.
Answer: option C
Explanation: verbs tenses

9.
Answer: option B
Explanation: the first word is the problem; the second word is the solution.

10.
Answer: option B
Explanation: the last letter of the word that is an "n" becomes an "l"

11.
Answer: option A
Explanation: to board means to get on a train. To mount means to get on a horse.

12.
Answer: option B
Explanation: feta is a Greek cheese, and mozzarella is an Italian cheese

13.
Answer: option C
Explanation: loafer is a type of shoe; moccasin is a type of snake.

14.
Answer: option D
Explanation: Nord is the opposite of Sud, and fear is the opposite of composure.

15.

Answer: option E

Explanation: mad is a synonym for insane, and obtuse is a synonym for stupid.

16.

Answer: option B

Explanation: the initial "I" is removed.

17.

Answer: option E

Explanation: to repair is an antonym of to damage. To segregate is an antonym of to unify.

18.

Answer: option B

Explanation: a monkey is a primate. An opossum is a marsupial.

19.

Answer: option A

Explanation: to singe means to char. To congeal means to solidify.

20.

Answer: option C

Explanation: a mouse is part of a computer. A flash is part of a camera.

21.

Answer: option D

Explanation: a king is a piece used in the game of chess. A shuttlecock is a piece used in the game of badminton.

22.
Answer: option A
Explanation: a forehand is an action in tennis. A swing is an action in golf.

23.
Answer: option C
Explanation: to inhale is more intense than to sniff. To lop is more intense than to snip.

24.
Answer: option E
Explanation: bean is a type of legume. Spelt is a type of wheat.

Verbal Classification Practice Test

p.134

1.
Answer: option D
Explanation: the last 3 letters are "ose".

2.
Answer: option A
Explanation: temperature, wind, humidity, and cloudiness are components, or parts, of weather.

3.
Answer: option C
Explanation: Akita, Australian Terrier, Barbet, and Basset Hound are dog breeds.

4.
Answer: option C
Explanation: Kimberlite, Pumice, Basalt, and Dacite are types of rocks.

5.
Answer: option B
Explanation: aspirin, paracetamol, ibuprofen, codeine are drugs

6.
Answer: option A
Explanation: nuclear, thermal, chemical, and kinetic are types of energy

7.
Answer: option C
Explanation: halogen, incandescent, led, and fluorescent are types of lightbulbs

8.
Answer: option D
Explanation: black, green, rooibos, oolong are types of tea.

9.
Answer: option C
Explanation: artificial, glacial, saline, and volcanogenic are types of lakes

10.
Answer: option D
Explanation: igloo, apartment, cottage, and villa are types of human houses.

11.
Answer: option A
Explanation: name, milk, baby, and gold are 4-letter words

12.
Answer: option C
Explanation: singular, plural, proper, and concrete are types of nouns.

13.
Answer: option D
Explanation: country, jazz, metal, and funk are types of music.

14.
Answer: option E
Explanation: small, class, press, and spell are words with double letters at the end..

15.
Answer: option A
Explanation: determiner, adverb, pronoun, and preposition are parts of speech.

16.
Answer: option C
Explanation: passive, linking, transitive, and intransitive are types of verbs.

17.
Answer: option B
Explanation: saw, used, drove, and wrote are past tense.

18.
Answer: option E
Explanation: combination, decomposition, combustion, and neutralization are chemical reactions.

19.
Answer: option C
Explanation: femur, patella, tibia, and fibula are leg bones

20.
Answer: option B
Explanation: angiosperms, deciduous, evergreens, and gymnosperms are types of trees.

Sentence Completion Practice Test
p.140

1.
Answer: option B
Explanation: caring=displaying kindness and concern for others.

2.
Answer: option C
Explanation: declared= formally asserted.

3.
Answer: option E
Explanation: grasp= seize and hold firmly.

4.
Answer: option A
Explanation: attempt = make an effort to achieve or complete something difficult.

5.
Answer: option C
Explanation: swallow = to take in; absorb.

6.
Answer: option D
Explanation: below= at a lower level.

7.
Answer: option D
Explanation: but= used to introduce a phrase or clause contrasting with what has already been mentioned.

8.
Answer: option A
Explanation: wisdom = the quality of having experience, knowledge, and good judgement.

9.
Answer: option C
Explanation: substitute = in place of.

10.
Answer: option C
Explanation: cell=the smallest structural and functional unit of an organism.

11.
Answer: option B
Explanation: narrower = limited in extent.

12.
Answer: option C
Explanation: great= of an extent, amount, or intensity considerably above average.

13.
Answer: option A
Explanation: assess = evaluate or estimate.

14.
Answer: option B
Explanation: attractive= pleasing or appealing to the senses.

15.
Answer: option C
Explanation: bind=stick together.

16.
Answer: option C
Explanation: breathing = the process of taking air into and expelling it from the lungs.

17.
Answer: option D
Explanation: keep= to stay in a particular place or condition.

18.
Answer: option E
Explanation: ultraviolet = describe light with a wavelength that's less than visible light, but longer than x-rays.

19.
Answer: option C
Explanation: rock = a large mass of stone.

20.
Answer: option D
Explanation: one complete orbit takes 365.256 days.

Figure Matrices Practice Test

p.149

1.
Answer: option A
Explanation: addition of a black dot and the figure becomes grey.

2.
Answer: option B
Explanation: the circle in the middle of the first row is removed.

3.
Answer: option D
Explanation: the left figure is rotated clockwise by 90 degrees and turns gray. 2 white circles are added diagonally.

4.
Answer: option C
Explanation: the figure on the left turns white. A diagonal is eliminated.

5.
Answer: option C
Explanation: the larger figure turns black. One of the 2 smaller figures is eliminated; the other is placed in the center of the larger figure.

6.
Answer: option E
Explanation: 2 windows are inserted in the left tower. The flags are removed.

7.
Answer: option B
Explanation: the figure on the right is the same as the one on the left with the addition of a 0.

8.
Answer: option A
Explanation: 180-degree rotation.

9.
Answer: option D
Explanation: the lower heart rotates by 90 degrees clockwise.

10.
Answer: option D
Explanation: the circle is removed.

11.
Answer: option D
Explanation: the gray oblique lines are removed and replaced with 4 gray circles.

12.
Answer: option B
Explanation: the right little figure goes to the left; the left little figure goes to the right but the circle is removed.

13.
Answer: option C
Explanation: 90 degree anticlockwise rotation.

14.
Answer: option E
Explanation: the upper element is removed; the lower element is rotated by 180 degrees.

15.

Answer: option E

Explanation: black circles increase by 2; black squares decrease by 1.

16.

Answer: option C

Explanation: the bottom element is placed on the top; the top element is placed in the middle and becomes gray; the middle element is placed at the bottom and becomes white.

17.

Answer: option D

Explanation: the figure is flipped horizontally; the pot changes shape and becomes white.

18.

Answer: option A

Explanation: the figure is flipped horizontally; the inside circle becomes a triangle.

19.

Answer: option C

Explanation: The figure rotates by 90 degrees clockwise.

20.

Answer: option D

Explanation: the shield changes shape; the figure in the shield rotates by 45 degrees clockwise.

21.

Answer: option D

Explanation: only the base of the crown changes in appearance.

22.
Answer: option A
Explanation: the figure rotates by 45 degrees counterclockwise; a horizontal line is added to the bottom of the figure.

Figure Classification Practice Test
p.158

1.
Answer: option A.
Explanation: same rotated figure consisting of a white triangle, a black triangle and a white rectangle.

2.
Answer: option B
Explanation: a large central white cross; 2 crosses placed along the left diagonal; a cross and a circle placed along the right diagonal.

3.
Answer: option D
Explanation: a white triangle, a grey circle, a black square.

4.
Answer: option B
Explanation: combos of 2 white rectangles,1 grey rectangle, 2 black triangles, a black circle, and a grey circle.

5.
Answer: option C
Explanation: same rotated figure; same colors.

6.
Answer: option E
Explanation: figures divided into 8 sections.

7.

Answer: option A

Explanation: same rotated figure.

8.

Answer: option E

Explanation: the hearts are all separated from each other.

9.

Answer: option C

Explanation: combos of a black and grey gift package with a black and white ribbon and a white heart pointing down.

10.

Answer: option E

Explanation: same rotated figure in different colors.

11.

Answer: option B

Explanation: a grey heart and a black heart; the black heart is partially hidden by the grey heart; the grey heart always points downward.

12.

Answer: option A

Explanation: combos of 3 hearts each divided in two halves; the heart with the black half on the right is always placed on top.

13.

Answer: option D

Explanation: the lower circle is the same as the upper circle but it is rotated by 45 degrees clockwise.

14.
Answer: option E
Explanation: the number of small circles equals the number of lines in the large circle.

15.
Answer: option A
Explanation: 9 squares: 5 white, 3 gray, 1 black. The black square is always in the top row.

16.
Answer: option B

Explanation: combos of a black square, a white square, a white triangle and a white circle.

17.
Answer: option D
Explanation: same image, consisting of a white and a gray part, rotated in different ways.

18.
Answer: option C
Explanation: the circles are divided into 8 equal slices; 2 white slices, 2 black slices, 4 grey slices. The 2 white slices are always in the same position.

19.
Answer: option B
Explanation: the number of legs equals the number of sides of the largest figure.

20.
Answer: option A
Explanation: each large figure contains 3 small figures different from itself.

21.
Answer: option D
Explanation: 2 black stylized little men; only the right one is always rotated.

22.
Answer: option E
Explanation: the number of larger circles is equal to the number of smaller black circles.

Paper Folding Practice Test
p.170

1.
Answer: option D

2.
Answer: option A

3.
Answer: option D

4.
Answer: option A

5.
Answer: option C

6.
Answer: option E

7
Answer: option A

8.
Answer: option D

9.
Answer: option B

10.
Answer: option A

11.
Answer: option E

12.
Answer: option C

13.
Answer: option E

14.
Answer: option C

15.
Answer: option A

16.
Answer: option A

Number Puzzle Practice Test
p.181

1.
Answer: option B
Explanation: 170-20=150; 150=150

2.
Answer: option A
Explanation: 110+860=970; 970=970

3.
Answer: option A
Explanation: 3244+212=3456; 3456=3456

4.
Answer: option E
Explanation: 9X21=625-436; 189=189

5.
Answer: option B
Explanation: 1002-31=945+26; 971=971

6.
Answer: option C
Explanation: 1123+131=5600-4346; 1254=1254

7.
Answer: option E
Explanation: 4136=9110-45-4929, 4136=4136

8.
Answer: option D
Explanation: 7477=6000-211+1688; 7477=7477

9.
Answer: option A
Explanation: 4012=1100+25+2887; 4012=4012

10.
Answer: option B
Explanation: 7137=8990-1853; 7137=7137

11.
Answer: option B
Explanation: 99+1180=4000-2721, 1279=1279

12.
Answer: option C
Explanation: 1760:4=650-210; 440=440

13.
Answer: option D
Explanation: 1300=3900:3; 1300=1300

14.
Answer: option A
Explanation: 210=14X15; 210=210

15.
Answer: option C
Explanation: 288=12X24; 288=288

16.
Answer: option D
Explanation: = 210+115; =325; 402=325+77; 402=402

Number Analogies Practice Test
p.187

1.
Answer: option E
Explanation: 72+1400=1472   5+1400=1405   9+1400=1409

2.
Answer: option A
Explanation: 1250:5=250   625:5=125   35550:5=7110

3.
Answer: option B
Explanation: 5160-59=5101   125-59=66   619-59=560

4.
Answer: option E
Explanation: 1569:3=523   126:3=42   729:3=243

5.
Answer: option D
Explanation: 805:5=161   950:5=190   355:5=71

6.
Answer: option B
Explanation: 93X5=465   41X5=205   27X5=135

7.
Answer: option A
Explanation: 42:7=6   77:7=11   777:7=111

8.
Answer: option A
Explanation: 4280:8=535   1888:8=236   384:8=48

9.
Answer: option C
Explanation: 15X2,5=37,5   8X2,5=20   11X2,5=27,5

10.
Answer: option D
Explanation: 224-13=211   1131-13=1118   129-13=116

11.
Answer: option C
Explanation: 17X4=68; 68-4=64   31X4=124; 124-4=120   13X4=52; 52-4=48

12.
Answer: option A
Explanation: 108:6=18   84:6=14   144:6=24

13.
Answer: option A
Explanation: 315:3,5=90   28:3,5=8   56:3,5=16

14.
Answer: option E
Explanation: 200:2=100; 100+10=110   30:2=15; 15+10=25   8:2=4 4+10=14

15.
Answer: option D
Explanation: 1000:4=250; 396:4=99; 220:4=55

16.

Answer: option C

Explanation: 600:3=200; 200+10=210   417:3=139: 139+10=149
918:3=306: 306+10=316

17.

Answer: option B

Explanation: 225:15=15   240:15=16   375:15=25

18.

Answer: option E

Explanation: 4X99=396; 7X99=693; 8X99=792

Number Series Practice Test
p.193

1.
Answer: option B
Explanation: -21, +15, -21, +15 etc.

2.
Answer: option C
Explanation: -54, +17, -54, +17 etc.

3.
Answer: option D
Explanation: -45, +46, -45, +46, etc.

4.
Answer: option A
Explanation: -5, +10, -3, -5, +10, -3, -5, etc.

5.
Answer: option C
Explanation: -403, +25, -403, +25, etc.

6.
Answer: option E
Explanation: -115, +1, +20, -115, +1, +20 etc.

7.
Answer: option B
Explanation: -59, +43, -59, +43, -59, etc.

8.
Answer: option A
Explanation: -15, +4, -6, -15, +4, -6, etc.

9.
Answer: option C
Explanation: +25, -36, +25, -36, +25, etc.

10.
Answer: option A
Explanation: +15, -6, +17, +15, -6, +17, etc.

11.
Answer: option E
Explanation: -23, +12, -23, +12, -23, +12, etc.

12.
Answer: option B
Explanation: -2, +15, 0, -2, +15, 0, etc.

13.
Answer: option D
Explanation: -25, -2, -6, -25, -2, -6, etc.

14.
Answer: option A
Explanation: +0.06, -0.04, +0.06, -0.04, +0.06, -0.04, etc.

15.
Answer: option D
Explanation: -0.12, +0.5, -0.12, +0.5, etc.

16.
Answer: option E
Explanation: -67, +2, -67, +2, -67, +2, etc.

17.
Answer: option C
Explanation: +5.5, -2, +5.5, -2, +5.5, -2, etc.

18.
Answer: option C
Explanation: -101, +25, -101, +25, -101, +25, etc.

Made in United States
Orlando, FL
21 October 2024

52998264R10128